HOW TO SELF-PUBLISH
COMICS
...NOT JUST CREATE THEM

JOSH BLAYLOCK

ISBN-13: 978-1-932796-67-4
ISBN: 1-932796-67-3

How to Self-Publish Comics...Not Just Create Them
SEPTEMBER, 2006. FIRST PRINTING. Published by Devil's Due
Publishing, Inc. Office of publication 4619 N. Ravenswood Ave. #204,
Chicago, IL 60640.

www.devilsdue.net

HOW TO SELF-PUBLISH
COMICS
...NOT JUST CREATE THEM

JOSH BLAYLOCK

SELECTED BOOKS BY DEVIL'S DUE PUBLISHING

CONTENTS

CHAPTER 1: Building the Infrastructure

CHAPTER 2: Building Your Creative Team

CHAPTER 3: Marketing and Production

CHAPTER 4: Hitting the Pavement

CHAPTER 1
Building the Infrastructure

INTRODUCTION

Since you've picked up this book, you have most likely at least pondered publishing your own comic, manga or graphic novel. Maybe you're a creator seeking a better understanding of the business of comics, so you don't get screwed somewhere down the line. I hope I can help you! Either way, you might be wondering, "Who the hell is this guy?"

I'll let you make up your mind on your own whether or not I'm someone you actually want to listen to, and either take this to the register, or quickly put it back on the shelf before the clerk yells that "this store ain't a library!"

I've finally surpassed the ten-year mark bouncing around this industry (and I've probably aged twenty years in that time), so I feel like I can actually pass on a bit of knowledge to help you enter the crazy world of comics, and maybe save you a few gray hairs in the process.

I wear a few hats, the largest of which is that of the president of Devil's Due Publishing, Inc.: the company which published this very text, and for which I'm most widely known. DDP, as our fans affectionately named us, is based out of Chicago, and we produce a variety of comics – everything from major licensed properties to wacky books about penguin superheroes and a little boy who turns into a werewolf. We're solidly listed in the Top Ten list of the industry's leading distributor, Diamond, and employ about a dozen key staff members at our hub. In addition, we employ anywhere from twenty to fifty freelance contractors at any given time. The company was founded in 1999 in Cincinnati, Ohio, and later officially incorporated in 2002 in the state of Illinois.

In 2004, I expanded the company to offer creative services, something I couldn't pass up, having access to so much amazing talent. We wouldn't become "agents" who find an artist, and then go hunting for work–instead, we'd hunt for the work, and then contact artists capable of handling the gig. In 2005, I officially spun that division off as a new entity, merging with another small firm that specialized in more corporate, conservative jobs: corporate websites, brand strategy… that kinda stuff. The new company is called Kunoichi, Inc., and does everything from websites for the US government and construction companies to toy designs and video game illustration.

Unrelated to the comics business, I've been dabbling in small real estate investments for the past couple of years, and plan to increase my efforts in that area in the future.

That's me in a nutshell. My hobby is my job is my life. It's all I really do, and I enjoy it. I guess you could say I'm addicted to it. In Donald Trump's book, *The Art of the Deal*, he wrote that most driven, or highly successful, people have a sort of "controlled neurosis" that they just manage to channel constructively. That sounds pretty close to the truth. I'm not your typical corporate type, which sometimes proves to be a challenge when dealing with those firmly entrenched in corporate America. Yet I have to confess that sometimes I like being underestimated. Maybe that's just me.

If I'm not working, I'm either finally getting around to catching a punk rock, psychobilly, hip hop or ska show, or hitting one of Chicago's many bars or clubs. Oh, or forcing myself into the gym, to make up for damaging myself at said bars and clubs. I wouldn't have it any other way right now. Maybe someday it'll be time to settle down, but right now I'm having too much fun.

The important thing is that it all started in 1995, with a few hundred bucks I saved from random crappy high school jobs, and a few more bucks I managed to borrow from my dad and my uncle. (Some would trace it back to the three little penguin toys my mom made for me when I was six that I felt compelled to draw stories about, adding guns and grenades in the mix. Or to my Dad's *Conan* comic collection, but I'd say that '95 was the official kick-off.)

Both of my parents came from very poor backgrounds financially, and my stepdad was from a hard-working, modest background. I got some help along the way, but I wasn't getting any free rides—the most my parents could offer me was encouragement, which they did in abundance. Don't get me wrong, I don't claim to have ever been poor—I was very well taken care of. As time went on, they really built nice lifestyles for themselves a hundred times better than what they started with. I was able to get some help through college, and spare cash here and there, but for the most part even if I could have it, I didn't want everything handed to me. I guess my parents succeeded in instilling in me that I needed to take care of myself at a young age.

Regardless, I knew from day one that I wanted to be in this line of work. I knew I wanted to draw, write, and create since before I could read, and pursued these pie-in-the-sky goals every day. I began to seek publishing opportunities long before I was skilled enough to be published and start

3

interacting with small press companies as early as age 14. I attended small local conventions, asked artists and self-publishers questions, and read everything I could find on the subject of breaking into comics. I received some great advice, but had some bad experiences as well.

By the time I was 18, I'd been misled and burnt by so many shady, fly-by-night types that I was compelled to blaze my own path. I pretty much devoted my entire life to that cause, and finally, at age 23, was able to go full time as a genuine comic book publisher. So although this success may have appeared to happen overnight, it was actually nine years in the making.

I'm focusing on all of the encouragement I had, but there was more than enough negativity thrown in my face every day. Lots of teachers and peers thought I had a "cute little dream" that would go away once reality set in.

Now maybe you're just looking at fulfilling a dream of producing a short comic book series and don't intend to quit your day job. Maybe, just like I was, you're almost obsessive about making it in this business. Either way, it's going to take an amazing amount of dedication to see it through.

Unless, that is, you're one of those one-in-a-million lucky bastards whom success seems to follow despite your lack of effort. Damn you people.

Just kidding…

…Well, only a little.

SOLICITATION INFORMATION

Your solicitation information is due to distributors about two months before their catalogs hits the stands. **SOLICITATION INFORMATION** is all of the information and graphics that are needed to inform people about your comic book. Meaning: the name of the writer and artist(s); price; frequency of publication; and an image of the cover. This means you need to know and have all of this content four months before your book is set to debut.

You can start to see how much money companies must invest in a comic book series before they begin to see a return.

About one month before your book's street date, you'll receive your orders from the distributor, explaining how many copies they wish to buy from you. This lets you know how many guaranteed sales you have. After judging how many reorder sales, convention sales, website sales, and promotional copies you anticipate needing, you'll be prepared to set your print run. It's important to have your computer files ready to go to the printer as soon as you get your orders. At Devil's Due, we usually have our files to the printer before we receive our orders, waiting to give the printer the "green light."

Your orders will arrive in the form of a **PURCHASE ORDER**. This is basically a promissory note that ensures you will be paid, as long as you deliver the product in time and as advertised. The purchase order contains important information to include in the instructions you send to your printer, because it gives them a breakdown of which warehouses to send comics to for each distributor. For example, Diamond has warehouses in Memphis, Tennessee, Plattsburgh, New York, and more, making it possible to get the books out to every store in the continent on the same day.

If you use Quebecor, the comic industry's largest print supplier, they actually have trucks that pick books up every Wednesday morning. Rather than paying to ship the books to Diamond, Diamond charges you a small percentage of the retail price of your book. Your check from them will be slightly smaller, but it's a very handy way to save some money on shipping costs, and a way to leverage their resources; i.e. you're not paying for shipping in advance, out of your own pocket.

So you've reached this point. Your comic is on the way to the shops, and your fingers are crossed, hoping it sells well enough that retailers reorder more, and that the next issue's advanced orders are higher.

Keep in mind: if you're doing a monthly publication, retailers will have to order the first three issues before they even receive issue one. This makes their orders much more conservative on issues one and two. For this reason, if you're a completely unknown creator or company, I suggest you consider releasing your comic on a bimonthly (once every two months), or even quarterly schedule at first. This allows more time for the comics to be purchased, and for word of mouth to circulate before issue two orders are due. Remember, most of your orders from comic shops are going to come from pull boxes.

Your check arrives about a month after the comics hit the stands, and you've now experienced every stage of publishing in the direct market. You are officially a comic book publisher.

A last but crucial note: Don't forget to invoice your distributors promptly! Some of them are good about paying you regardless, but you run the risk of not getting paid until 30 days after they receive your invoice, rather than your books. If you go a month without billing them, expecting your money, you may be in for a rude awakening. At the end of this issue is a sample of a basic Purchase Order. There are a number of very inexpensive accounting software packages these days to help you keep track of your expenses and income... although paper and pencil still work too!

DISTRIBUTION

BOOK MARKET

When distributing your comic books through bookstores, there are a lot of distributors out there. Diamond Book Distributors is one, and is a division separate from Diamond Comic Distributors, with different support staff.

Other options are CDS, Baker & Taylor, Amazon.com, Hastings, Ingram, and on and on. You can also sell to the major chains like Borders and Barnes & Noble. Devil's Due uses Diamond, so that is where the majority of my knowledge comes from. Diamond sub-distributes via many of the smaller distributors mentioned above. Again, you need to do what best makes sense for you.

Here are a few key points about the **BOOK MARKET**:

- The Book Market is made up of key buyers for large chains.
- Book Market catalogs solicit months and months ahead—up to a year in advance—unlike the Direct Market's shorter four to five month window.
- The Book Market in general has a much larger percentage of female readers than the Direct Market, and a younger audience overall.

- The Book Market works heavily off of "backlist" sales, which means you can make even more money over the long term than right up front.
- The Catch-22 of the Book Market is that you can reach every major store in the country by selling to a select few chain buyers—but if those few buyers don't like your product, you're unlikely to get in those stores. The moral of the story: don't piss anyone off.

It's very important to get to know the sales and marketing staff of your Book Market distributor. They are the ones who directly communicate with the buyers on a frequent basis, and they have hundreds of titles to sell, not just yours.

NEWSSTAND

NEWSSTAND is the avenue of distribution for **PERIODI-CALS** (i.e.: monthly comics or magazines) such as the magazine rack at your local grocery store, or the comics you find in convenient stores. Even the comics and magazines on sale at bookstores, such as Borders, are considered newsstand, and are accounted separate from their more book-like counterparts, the graphic novel.

Newsstand is a whole other ball game, and one that I'm still learning about every day. In some ways, dealing with these distributors has made me appreciate Diamond more, although I'm still excited about the opportunities that the newsstand offers. It is not something I would recommend to someone just starting out, though. Newsstand, like the Book Market, is 100% returnable.

ONLINE STORE

When you're beginning your first comic book or manga publishing endeavor, it's just a reality that it's going to be tough getting your book placed in stores. You need every penny you can get from these comics, and more importantly, a place that customers can always find your product.

How many times have you been interested in a manga, magazine, or CD only to find that the stores in your area don't carry them? Do you pursue them after a couple of tries? After one try? Most likely not, unless you're already a big fan. That's why your online web store is so important. Can't do a full service web store yet? Get an E-Bay account and list items with the "buy it now" feature. It's no comparison to a true online shop, but it will get you moving in the right direction.

One way to increase revenues from web sales, and make visiting your site more worth your readers' time, is to offer subscriptions. It's hard enough to earn readers, so once you do, reel them in for the long term. A four- or six-issue subscription not only brings you more money, but it guarantees they'll stick around to read your whole story.

Of course, you must be very responsible if you sell subscriptions. The last thing you want to do is spend a customer's money, and then find that you won't be continuing your series past the second issue. You'll end up owing some very unhappy people a lot of money.

Above all, remember that your webstore is not merely a sub-page on your website. It is the nexus of your website. The only reason your website exists is to market and sell your product. Every aspect of it should help to achieve this goal.

KNOW YOUR KINKO'S

Ahh, the local copy center. Whether it's Kinko's, Office Max, or just Billy Bob's Big Beautiful Copies up the street, you want to know the employees at these shops: they are your best friends.

It's been a few years since I really needed to use a copy center; Devil's Due prints so many copies for printer mock-ups and general daily business use that it became much more cost effective for us to lease a full service hi-tech copier/scanner a long time ago. But I remember my copy center days vividly. I even worked at a Kinko's for awhile during art school.

You're going to need to make copies for all sorts of reasons, and maybe even produce promotional mini-comics (called **ASHCANS**) once you complete enough of your first issue.

Most of you reading this are probably already smirking from your own experiences spending long nights using the sweet Mac Design Station set-up at the copy shop where your friend works on third shift (which you still pay for, of course). I think Kinko's is a rite of passage for pretty much every comic artist and publisher out there.

Another option is to take advantage of your high school, college, or job facilities if your superiors are supportive of your self-publishing efforts. Either way, there's no way to publish efficiently these days without some decent computer equipment and copy capabilities, so make sure you know where you're going to have access to them.

DISTRIBUTOR WARS!

The distribution scenario was not always like it is today. Once, long ago, in the era known as the '80s, there were many many small distributors. Like any business, they began to consolidate as the more efficient companies bought out the smaller companies, or put them out of business via competition. When I first started to educate myself on this subject in 1991, as an ambitious ninth grader, there were about a dozen distributors.

By the mid nineties, that number narrowed to just a scant few serious players. Heroes World, Friendly Frank's, Capital, and Diamond, were some of the largest distributors during the comics boom of the '90s, when small press publishers were selling tens of thousands of copies of amateur black and white product. Marvel, DC, Dark Horse, and the newly formed Image Comics were selling millions of copies every month.

That's when Marvel decided they were so big that they didn't need a distributor. They were going to distribute themselves. They acquired Heroes World, and were converting it into a Marvel-only distributor. Suddenly the industry was abuzz with chatter. Friendly Frank's went out of business, and we were left with three giant distribution powerhouses.

Then something happened that took everyone by surprise. From what I understand, feeling they needed their own special distribution deal to compete, DC Comics signed a major exclusive contract with Diamond. In that instant, the distribution wars hit nuclear level. I remember wondering, even at the age of 16, why on Earth DC would do such a thing: they could have been the darlings of the industry, and had the might of every distributor, while Marvel struggled to go it alone.

In hindsight, I can now see where they were coming from, although anyone paying attention could foresee that Marvel was not likely going to succeed. I think it was a knee-jerk, shortsighted move, and definitely not the best decision for the industry. That's when Capital was forced to make a move and try to acquire its own exclusive publishers. Kitchen Sink and Viz signed with Capital, and now, in order to receive all of the top product in the market, store managers were forced to order from all three distributors, whereas they had previously been able to use just one if they so desired.

The loss of both Marvel and DC was too great, though, and Capital shut its doors in 1996, negotiating a deal with Diamond. It was now down to Diamond and Heroes World.

Meanwhile, Marvel wasn't faring so well with the distribution venture. To put it delicately, they fell flat on their face, and came crawling back, only to find an industry with very few, if any, alternative choices for quality distribution. They signed their deal with Diamond, and remain exclusive with them for the Hobby/Collector shops to this day. For an even more in-depth, and very fascinating, look into the Marvel Comics of the 1990s, read a book called *Comic Wars* by Dan Raviv, available in most bookstores and comic shops.

So this is why, when you're flipping through the Previews catalog every month, you see those top four premier vendors ahead of everyone else in the catalog. As most people, including myself, understand it, these publishers have been grandfathered in with their exclusive agreements. Will they ever leave? It's doubtful. There would have to be a viable alternative in place for them to do so, and as long as they are exclusive, it's hard for any aspiring distributors to sustain themselves. It's a Catch-22 any way you look at it.

Does this make Diamond the "Big Bad Corporation"? Absolutely not. They were simply the victors in the process of capitalism. Many contest that they are a monopoly, and it was even investigated by the federal government. The case was subsequenty dropped.

Do I wish there was a little more competition? It'd be nice, but you have to work within the reality you live. Devil's Due has an exclusive contract with Diamond as well. It just makes sense. We have a very strong relationship with them, and work closely with our account reps and their sales and marketing staff regarding all of our product. Sometimes being the only guy on the block makes them easy prey for unsatisfied customers, though.

(Covered my rear there, whew!)

WITH THE FOUNDATION IN PLACE, YOU MAY NOW BUILD!

If you've made it this far, congratulations! You have laid the foundation of the publishing infrastructure that you and your creative team will need to get your product out into the market. This is no small feat. By doing this, and not just blindly drawing or writing away, hoping your comic will magically get published, you're ahead of about 80% of all other aspiring self-publishers. You're on your way to introducing your manga or comic to the world.

Maybe after all your research, and adding the numbers, you've decided this is not the route you want to take. Maybe you'd prefer to simply focus on the creative side of things. Well, congratulations to you as well! You just saved yourself months of headaches, and potentially thousands of dollars. Did you know, though, that most creators have no idea how the comics they create actually make it to the stands? It's shocking how little many know; even some thirty-year comics veterans are clueless to the publishing and distribution side of the industry. By educating yourself and putting in a little extra time on the side, you're better prepared to create comics professionally. You will have an understanding of your editors' and publishers' points of view which most creators fail to learn.

The next step in the publishing game is Marketing, followed by the creative process. "*Followed* by creative?" you may ask. Well, not always, but even though they are almost simultaneous events, you want to make sure you have your marketing infrastructure firmly in place so that you'll be able to keep up your promotional efforts without getting caught up in the creative work. Creative work is a black hole that loves to suck you in, and keep you from maintaining the business side of things.

That's one of my personal strong points. And before it sounds like I have a big head, and even worse, that my big head's up my ass, let me say I am not an amazing talent. I consider myself a pretty good artist when I really have the time to focus, and a solid writer, but I'm also able to tackle these chores while focusing on the business. The older I get, the more I realize that that ambidextrous ability to perform the left-brain/right-brain tag team is actually a unique ability. Usually it's one or the other. It's an old stereotype, but it really does seem that the more talented the creator, the more flakey they can be in terms of business. Then, when you're dealing with a guy right out of corporate America with an MBA in business management, he often doesn't have a creative bone in his body.

Even still, it is very difficult to switch gears during the day, jumping back and forth from creative writing or drawing to spreadsheets and administrative duties. It's just very difficult, because your brain needs a little while to get into the creative mindset, or into the groove. Whenever I write, I have to go hide away at a coffee shop or on my condo building's rooftop room—anywhere away from distractions. If you can do both, even simultaneously, then take that talent and run with it. You've got me beat!

My point is, it's OK to know what your strong points are, because knowing your strong points also means knowing your weak points. Are you that talented artist who can't even balance your own checkbook? Then get a partner who can! Are you the accountant who's always loved comics, but deep down inside, you know you're not a good writer? Don't let your own ego stand in the way of making a good comic. Hire someone who is great, and have him/her expand upon your ideas. Everyone, even you, will be much happier with the end product.

"But Josh," you're thinking. "I know I'm not that great, but it's what I really really want to do. The whole reason I'm self-publishing is because I want to be an artist. I just need more practice." Well then, by all means keep up your efforts to achieve your dream—but ask yourself again: why are you self-publishing? It's very time consuming, expensive, and draining. If you take another year to improve your talents before publishing, you'll have a product to be proud of, and never have to look back on those memories thinking, "my God, what was I doing back then?" Trust me, I speak from personal experience! Ever heard of my first comic book, *Minotaur*? Probably not, and there's a good reason.

CLOSING

Sometimes my comments or advice sound harsh, or even mean, and that's the opposite of my intentions. This can be a tough industry, and if you jump into it without thinking, trust me that it will be a lot harsher than I've ever been. I'd like to help ensure that your publishing experience is as exciting and fulfilling as possible.

This is exactly how I treat myself. I don't sugarcoat things, or try to paint a pretty picture when there isn't one. I think everyone who works for me knows I can't stand someone tiptoeing around a problem, and appreciate an honest assessment of the situation. There simply isn't time to pussyfoot around issues. We call it like it is, and deal with the challenges that we face head on. What's great is that when you succeed, you know it's for real. And that's the best feeling of all.

Whether you continue reading this entire book or decide to venture into the publishing arena from this point, good luck to you. I hope my prattling on has helped in some small way. Now get out there and start building your infrastructure. Make me regret writing this five years from now, when I wish I could publish you, but you're already doing too well on your own to accept my offer!

CHAPTER 2
Building Your Creative Team

Building Your Creative Team

INTRODUCTION

Whether you've decided to publish your own comic or manga, or are going to publish through someone else's company, hopefully this will help you to be as informed as possible. There's no comparison to real life experience, but consider this your "debriefing"—and hey, that's way more than most people get before diving headfirst into the industry. So, congratulations to you for seeking the information out in the first place.

Although some people attempt to create an entire comic book by themselves, most people form a team of creators. This team may consist of any combination of writers, artists, and designers. Often times these are two or three friends, eager to break into comics.

We're going to explore the various facets of building up the creative team who will produce your comic or manga publication. However, we're not going to dwell on the creative process. Here, we focus on the legal and administrative responsibilities that go into it.

Anyone can gather a team of artists and writers to help create a comic book, but too often young publishers do not take their agreements with these creators to a professional level: the contract stage. Many people are intimidated by the legal process—an average attorney in Chicago, home to DDP, charges anywhere from $250 to $300 per hour, so I can understand the hesitation. However, once you have a boiler-plate in place, it is easy to make changes yourself. **BOILER-PLATE** is the term commonly used for a template of text that basically stays the same with each agreement you sign, with a few small changes for the specific deal.

Even if you don't go to an attorney to draft your agree-ment, any information you can gather to document the terms of your deal is useful: emails, text message conversations, handwritten agreements on toilet paper… anything. Later, I will discuss the steps in making an agreement from scratch, and minimizing your legal fees.

Let me preface this by stressing that I am not an attorney. I'm not even a part-time paralegal. I've just had a lot of expe-rience working with creators and have drafted a number of contracts ranging from standard work for hire deals to multi-year licensing terms with major corporations. "What's work for hire?" you ask. That's why we're spending a whole chapter on this subject. You, and only you, are responsible for any legal agreement you may enter into. I am only here to offer my opinion.

I still consult my attorneys on a regular basis, and suggest you do the same if you are at all uncertain, or are inexperi-enced in reading or drafting contracts.

YOUR CREATIVE TEAM

Comic books require a set of very specific talents to be created: a writer, penciller, inker, colorist, and letterer. As I've said before, there are many great books on the market that explain these roles in detail, but I'm trying to focus on the business side of their relationships with you, the publisher, so I'll be brief. For the sake of us all being on the same page, the following is a breakdown of a comic book creative team:

The Writer: This is the person who actually drafts the script for your story. S/He may be working from a concept initiated by someone else, or creating something from scratch. Some writers are very descriptive, and specifically break down the scene and dialogue for every single panel to be drawn on every page. Others have a looser style, and prefer to give the artist a rough outline of what is happening on each page, fitting the dialogue in later.

The Penciller: The artist who brings the script to life is the penciller, so called because s/he depends on just that: a pencil. This artist must interpret the writer's descriptions and ensure that they are visually translated onto the paper. The

penciller designs the structure of the panels on the page. Not only that, but they must be able to show emotion in the character's expressions and body language. Basically, a comic book penciller must be able to draw anything, from any angle, and typically needs to produce a page a day to make a decent living (in North America, anyway).

The Inker: Inkers must trace over the art drafted by the penciller, making sure to maintain clean, crisp lines, and when called for, add depth and weight to the art. The inker needs to take care that everything doesn't look flat and two-dimensional; backgrounds should appear to fade into the distance, and the foreground should pop out at the reader. At one time, inking was vital to the process, because printing technology was limited, but with computers, artists are finally breaking the rules. I've seen all sorts of pencil/ink combinations, and there is some amazing art out there, so your artists are not as limited as they once would have been. Inking, however, is probably the most abused facet of the art form. Many people think it's easy, but good pencils can be destroyed by poor inks.

Oh, and if you ever meet an inker in person, please refrain from the all-too-often-heard "tracer" joke popularized by the movie *Chasing Amy*. Not because the artist will take himself too seriously, but because those jokes were funny ten years ago, and have all the relevance of a knock-knock joke these days. (I say this less out of concern for inkers than from my selfish desire to never hear that joke again. Say it with me, "played out!")

The Colorist: Colorists add hue, tone, and depth to the black and white inked artwork. The art of coloring has

changed more than any other facet of the comics form. Once upon a time a colorist's palette and capabilities were extremely affected by the limits of the printing process, and coloring was mainly very flat and featureless. Computers have changed all that—colorists are often very involved in the rendering of the page, employing complex shading, multiple light sources, modeled shapes, and a plethora of other tools once unavailable.

Particularly in the area of colors, the Internet has allowed us to see what the rest of the world has to offer, and there is an amazing pool of talent out there. Devil's Due, for instance, uses colorists from the United States, Canada, South Korea, Malaysia, and Italy.

The Letterer: Comics these days are virtually all lettered via the computer as well, using programs like Adobe Illustrator and InDesign. The letterer takes the computer art files and the original script and builds those words into custom-shaped word balloons on each panel. Way back in the Twentieth Century—like 1995—lettering was largely done by hand. Today, there are a number of fonts your letterer can employ to give your comic's dialogue that "comic book" feel.

It still takes a good set of design skills to letter properly, and even though I'm not a pro letterer, let me save you from making a grave mistake right now: never use the fonts that come stock with your PC or Mac computer, or comic fonts that have been around since the dawn of digital lettering. Keep your fonts fresh. And seriously: if you use the font Comic Sans, cut up your printouts and start over. If you don't understand why that's a bad thing, that's okay—you just shouldn't be the one lettering. Go find yourself a letterer.

CONTRACT, CONTRACT, CONTRACT

The most important reason you sign contracts with people is to ensure that everyone has a clear understanding of their role in the publishing process. I don't know who first said it, but the saying I always remember is, "Contracts are for when things go *bad*, not when they're going good." Over time, even the simplest agreement can be misunderstood as memory fade and selective memory takes over. Many a friendship has been lost over scenarios like this. If you have an agreement in writing, no one can argue with it.

Before I "went pro," I heard plenty of artists claim that they "don't like to worry about contracts." Boy, are those guys in for a world of hurt someday. No one wants to think that current relationships could sour years later, because no one feels that their current partners would intentionally try to burn them. The truth is: it's true, that's very unlikely. Instead, what happens is that with the passing of time, people forget what was said—or worse, each person had a different understanding of the agreement to begin with, because it was too vague.

An example: you are the "business-minded" person on your team, and you agree verbally that you will "split the profits fifty-fifty." What if your definition of "profits" is different from your partner's? Your parnter may think that "profit" means all of the sales from the book, while you (correctly) define "profit" as all sales after costs for shipping, printing, advertising, etc. That's a huge difference. Let's add a complication: this misunderstanding isn't even realized until six months after you and your partner start working together…because that's when the first check arrives from the distributor. Now you have a partner who is very frustrated and may feel that you are going back on your word.

If you are able to refer to a contract that clearly states and defines the meaning of "profits" in this relationship—a contract signed by all parties involved—this problem is quickly resolved. Your partner may still be upset or frustrated, but the contract you both signed will have served its purpose: you both agreed, in advance, to a certain statement, and thus adhering to the contract allows both of you to maintain your integrity, and know that no one's trying to pull a fast one.

UNDERSTAND EVERYONE'S GOALS

I spend a good deal of time writing about this in this book, but it bears repeating: *What do you want out of this?* This is not just a question to ask yourself, but to ask your partners. Are you very serious about making a professional living in the comic book industry or just fulfilling a childhood dream for kicks? It's important that you partner with someone who shares your goals.

For instance, if you are drop-dead serious and highly motivated about writing a professional manga, but you team up with an artist who is only halfheartedly involved and not willing to put as much effort into the venture as you are, you should know this up front. Perhaps you assume that the artist is going to help you promote your venture online, that s/he's going to help pay for tables at conventions, and do as much to market the product as you are. Yet s/he may just be drawing the comic for fun. S/He may draw an incredible-looking comic, but if everyone's expectations are not in sync, it can cause serious problems very quickly.

Say your main goal with your self-published comic book is to get the attention of someone like the senior editor at Devil's Due, and score a job writing fantasy comics? What if your artist has decided that s/he only wants to draw in an *Invader Zim* style? Your writing may be great, but your sample product won't be in line with the genre you're trying to get hired for.

What if you're an artist, and you're serious about sticking it out with a series for a full year, but the writer you team with only wants to write for a few issues—or worse, you want a serious action story, and s/he's set on filling it with jokes?

Every one of these scenarios may seem painfully obvious. You may be reading each paragraph and saying, "Blaylock's new name is Captain Obvious!" But those are some of the most common and most serious mistakes many people make when publishing. Hell, those are some of the biggest mistakes people make in major life decisions, period. Clashing goals can be a major setback.

©, ®, AND ™

Before we get into the section on Work for Hire, it's important to know just what the terms **COPYRIGHT** and **TRADE-MARK** mean. They are commonly used, but few people understand the difference. The intricacies of these laws are worthy of their own book, and many have written about them, but the basic concept is pretty simple:

COPYRIGHT

If you own the copyright to something, it means, basically, that you have the right to copy it, to reproduce it in any medium. For example, you've created a character named Jimmy AllPowerful, and asked me to draw a picture of him. I agree to do so for free, and tell you that you may publish it as a pin-up in one of your comic books. Although you created the character, I own the copyright on that image. If you want to use that image in another comic book, or on a T-shirt, you must again ask me for permission. If you're selling a lot of comics, I'm probably going to want some money.

Notice: I still do not own the character, just the image I drew of it. That's because you own the trademark. If I took that image, and produced T-shirts of it without your permission, you would have just cause to make me stop (or as they love to say, "cease and desist").

Most states have laws that automatically protect your creations the very moment you put pen to paper, or fingers to keyboard. However, it never hurts to mount the evidence in your favor, so it's a good idea to officially copyright your work through the government.

The symbol used to identify copyright ownership is ©. To type this on your computer, simply type "*alt-G*". Contrary to popular belief, you do not have to register your art or text with the government to place a copyright symbol on it. Registration with the state or federal government simply helps strengthen your claim of ownership in court.

TRADEMARK

Trademark is the ownership of more than just an image: it's basically the ownership of an idea. It is the general concept, and all of the associated characteristics that go along with it. It's really hard to explain, but once you understand, the concept of "trademark" should be very simple.

The US Government breaks trademarks into categories and various media. For instance, Superman is a term that's been around a lot longer than the DC comic book everyone knows today. The concept of a hero in tights and a cape is also a very general concept that no one person can claim to own. Krypton is an actual element on the periodic table of elements. Lastly, the letter "S" is simply a part of the alphabet, and free for everyone to use. Put them all together, though, and you have a trademark.

DC's Superman is a powerful hero from the planet Krypton, wearing blue and red tights and a cape, with a very unique "S" design on his chest—and these are some of the details that comprise the trademark of Superman. Even more specifically, this trademark applies to comic books. Now, Superman has been around for a zillion years, and has been merchandised into many other media, and DC (or their parent company Warner Bros.) has taken care to register the "tm" in various categories. You still hear the term "Superman" in songs, though, and there's nothing DC can do about it unless the song refers to very specific elements of their character's trademark.

The universal symbol for Trademark is simply "tm," seen somewhere on most logos and product packaging. Just like copyrights, if you have created something, you have every right to place a "tm" by its name.

REGISTERED COPYRIGHT

This is the big daddy of copyright and trademark law. If you see any product with an ® ("*alt*-R" on your keyboard), that means the owner has officially registered it with the Library of Congress. They've sent images, text descriptions, and logos to the Feds, and paid a few hundred bucks to do so, to ensure they protect their property as best as possible.

Again, I must reiterate that I am not an attorney, and you should seek professional advice on the subject, but this gives us a start.

WORK-FOR-HIRE VS. CREATOR-OWNED

When starting your comic book publishing venture, you need to decide up front: is this going to be something that you own outright, or will you share in the ownership of rights with your creators? Sharing a percentage of sales is different than sharing ownership.

In 1976 the United States Government passed a bill that clarified the copyright issues, and created the "Work for Hire" clause. Depending on your view of creative rights, this may be positive or negative, but what it allows one to do is retain all of the copyright for any artwork or stories created by someone else. The rule is that the artist must agree to this, and sign an agreement saying so.

This is how large companies like Disney can have thousands of people working for them, drawing and writing stories, but maintain ownership of everything.

What this does not cover is the ownership of the original artwork. Traditionally, the artist keeps the physical art, which s/he may then sell. However, if s/he's signed a work for hire agreement, they do not necessarily have permission to reproduce it or to allow anyone else to.

On the flip side, if you do not sign a WFH agreement, the artist owns the copyright to the work. It's only by his/her permission that someone else may publish it beyond the one-time usage he's being paid for. Even if you've published the art, you must get permission to produce it a second time, or to use pieces of the art on T-shirts, stickers, or anything else.

An example of the work for hire clause would read as such:

> *The Work created hereunder has been specially*
> *commissioned by Devil's Due to use as contribution*
> *to a collective work, and constitutes a work made for*

*hire as that is used in the United States Copyright
Act of 1976. Talent acknowledges that s/he has been
engaged to perform hereunder. In the event the Work
is deemed not to be a work made for hire, the Talent
hereby assigns to Devil's Due all rights in the works,
including copyright and trademark rights and all
other rights to exploit the work in all media now or
hereafter existing throughout the world in eternity.*

Now, when starting out, it's very common to agree to
share ownership of the copyright and trademarks of your
comics. Many split the ownership 50/50. If you're the
publisher, for instance, your contribution may involve paying
for and managing the business aspects of publishing, while
the creators are putting their time into working for you, most
likely for little or no pay.

PAYMENT TERMS: PAGE RATES, ROYALTIES, AND COMP COPIES

Among the top-selling comic book publishers, writers are
paid by the page (known as a page rate), as are artists and
letterers. These rates can range from $50 a page to $250 a
page, depending on the level of talent.

When it comes to self-publishing, however, unless
you have significant amounts of disposable cash, you won't
be coughing up that kind of dough. If you're not writing
the book yourself, what is often done is to offer the writer
a percentage of the profits. Of course, it's wisest to make
sure you have someone who is working out of a love of the
medium, and for exposure. Chances are, you're not going to
sell enough to make any money back – you're doing this for
the experience, but there's always a chance you'll create the
next *Bone* or *Teenage Mutant Ninja Turtles*, so you want to dot

your I's and cross your T's.

It's important to determine what "percentage of profits" means, and to get it in writing. Remember, contracts are for when things go wrong, not right. As time passes, memories become selective, and good friends may begin to fight over money. A well-drafted contract, even if it's only an email agreement, can save you a world of problems later (see next section, "Drafting a Contract (and Saving Money)") I've included a sample document of a basic writer/publisher agreement, based on shared profits.

Sometimes a person will believe "profits" or "net sales" to mean "money left over after all printing costs." Meanwhile, his/her partner understands profits to be money left over after paying for printing, shipping, advertising, website hosting, supply costs, gas money and printer cartridges. See how easily that can be misunderstood? The worst scenario that can happen is that you could be losing a couple thousand dollars, and your writer or artist believes you're hoarding a lion's share of cash.

Another option for payment based on sales is offering a flat royalty for each issue sold. This means that whether you make or lose money, the talent will be paid a flat price for each copy of the book that is sold. For example, you and your writer agree that you will pay 5% of the cover price. If you sell 3,000 copies of a $3.00 book, the total sales would be $9,000. Thus, your writer is then owed $450 (9,000 x .05 = 450)

Be sure when drafting a royalty agreement that you specify **COVER PRICE** or **WHOLESALE COST**. If you agreed to pay 5% of wholesale, a $3.00 product would sell to distributors for around $1.20 (that's $3.00 minus a 60% discount to the distributor, or $3.00 x .4 = $1.20). Five percent of the wholesale cost of 3,000 books would be $180. That's way off from $450, and a confused writer will not be happy.

If you're new to this idea of payment (or if you just plain hate math), it may seem a little intimidating, but take some time to digest it. It's all very simple arithmetic. Practice a few scenarios on paper, and see if you get the hang of it.

You can stay simple, or get as creative as you want with the deal. Here's a possible scenario for a publisher:

Clyde McWriterpants agrees to script a four-issue mini-series of *Super-Hypo-Force 3000*. The publisher is going to pay him $50 per page, for each 22-page issue. That means he's going to receive $1100 per issue. Now, McWriterpants is an established pro, and his rate at another publisher is $85 a page, so he's not doing this for the money, he just likes working with the publisher. Still, if the book does well, he wants to make sure he enjoys his share of the wealth. So the publisher agrees that in addition to the page rate, Clyde will receive a 10% royalty on the wholesale cost of the book, after sales break 10,000 copies.

Follow me?

Super-Hypo-Force 3000 debuts, and it's a surprise hit, selling 20,000 copies. Clyde was already paid his page rate of $50 per page, a total of $1100, but now he's entitled to 10% of the wholesale on all copies sold after the first 10,000. In this case, it's easy math: 20,000 copies, minus 10,000, and we are left with 10,000 copies. The comic sold for $3.00, making the wholesale price $1.20. That means the publisher receives $12,000 for those additional sales, and now owes Clyde 10% of that, or $1200. Not bad for Clyde. Since he was willing to take a risk, he's now raked in $2300, which breaks down to over $104 a page.

If you're like most people starting out, and need to find creators to work for little pay up front, you may still be able to spare one expense that could add a very professional touch to your comic: you can hire an established pro to create your covers.

I'm not suggesting you run out and pay super-hot artist J. Lee Scott Campbell Ross $2500 to draw a cover, but someone who's currently drawing comics for the bigger companies gives readers the perception that your book is of the same quality.

Don't tell anyone I told you, but often times the pros will draw the cover for you at a major discount, just because they enjoy helping out the new guys. Be sure to offer him/her something, though, even if it's buying drinks at the next convention. You never know: five years later you might be able to return the favor, and hire the same artist for real pay.

DRAFTING A CONTRACT (AND SAVING MONEY)

Writing a contract seems like a very intimidating task, but just like the creation of a comic book, it's done step by step, and with help from your team. It all starts with a simple conversation: what do you want out of the deal and what are your team members expecting? This needs to be done on a one-on-one basis with each member. After talking, you can begin to jot down notes about all of the various terms. It helps to know what questions to ask, so hopefully I can help by providing a scenario:

Sean has decided that he wants to publish a comic book called *Ninja Pants: the Domination*. He believes it's the best idea in the world, and must be published. He has thoroughly thought about why he wants to do it, and received honest criticism from others about his professional level, and it was positive.

Sean is going to write *Ninja Pants* himself, but does not want to, or cannot draw it, because he only knows how to draw with crayons. He's pretty good at lettering and graphic design, though, so he's going to handle that part himself.

Sean isn't interested in publishing this book for years and years, but instead wants to use it as a resume piece to show to bigger publishers. So this comic is just going to be a one-shot, self-contained story.

Sean has found an artist named Caitlin, who is awesome at drawing in a manga style, and perfect for *Ninja Pants: the Domination*. She too is just looking for an opportunity to get her work seen by the "big guys," so this is perfect for her.

When they finally discuss the arrangement, Sean and Caitlin have their questions ready to go (they've already read my book, so they knows what to ask):

1. If I can't pay you any money up front, are you willing to work for a percentage of the profits? Is 50/50 fair?

2. How quickly can you create a penciled and inked page of comic book art, and how much free time do you have to work on it?

3. How will you deliver art to me, and can you send images to me at various stages, such as sketch, pencils, and then finally inks?

4. What do you think is a fair amount of revisions to do for each page?

5. How much money will be used for advertising and will it be considered one of the expenses when you calculate profits?

6. How do you define "profits"?

7. How long does it take to get money from the distributor, and other customers, and when will we receive our first checks?

8. Who is retaining ownership of the Ninja Pants title and characters? If the artist does all of the designs, does she keep partial rights?

9. Do all of these terms apply to future printings of the book?

10. What if someone wants to make a T-shirt, movie, podcast, cell-phone download, or other merchandise based on the comic book art? How do we split the income?

11. If we promote this book at conventions, how is the money divided? Who is going to pay for the booth rental at the conventions?

12. If a lot of work is done on the comic book, but the entire project is cancelled for any reason, what happens? Is anyone owed any money? Do the division of ownership rights change?

From there, Sean and Caitlin are off to a pretty good start. These questions beget more questions, and by the time they are all answered, they'll have a pretty solid contract. The process of putting these together in a rough draft results in a **DEAL MEMO** or **LETTER OF INTENT**. Basically, the deal memo is what you write up in your own words, that you both agree to, before passing it along to an attorney.

Obviously, if you involved the attorney in the process any earlier, it would have cost a lot more. Now, depending on your experience level and writing abilities, you may be able to take this a little further on your own. I usually go beyond the deal memo, and once it's agreed upon, draft a full contract. This is where I try to conceive of every single circumstance that could possibly happen, and include it in the document. I'm almost 30, though, and have been writing agreements since I was 16, so I've had some practice. I don't recommend it for someone just starting out.

I've finally done this enough that, if a new deal is very similar to deals I've done in the past, I may choose not to send it to my attorney. However, if it's at all unfamiliar territory, I email it to him right away. The consequences of making a mistake are just too risky. I've usually typed things out so much, though, that it take him less than an hour to review and amend the document.

Following is an example of a sample contract for Sean and Caitlin's deal. Feel free to use this as inspiration, but please do not copy it word for word. I'm only doing this for the purposes of the book, and again, stress that I am NOT a licensed attorney.

The basic breakdown of categories I start with, after assessing all of the questions each party has, are length of **TERM**, each party's **COMMITMENTS**, **PAYMENT** terms, **OWNERSHIP** rights, and **TERMINATION** details.

PAYMENT AGREEMENT: SAMPLE CONTRACT

NINJA PANTS: THE DOMINATION

This Agreement ("Agreement") is effective as of this XX day of XXXX, 200X (the "Effective Date") by and between Caitlin ("Creator") and Sean ("Publisher").

Term

This agreement shall be effective for two years from the date of execution. Upon expiration of the term, the agreement must be renegotiated, and does not automatically renew, with the exception of specific clauses that may obligate Creator or Publisher to share in responsibilities, payment distribution, or rights ownership for a longer period of time.

No terms of this agreement may be changed without a written amendment agreed to by both parties, executed via signed contract, or email confirmation.

Commitment

Publisher agrees to produce *Ninja Pants: The Domination* (the Comic), a forty-eight page comic book story, to be distributed through comic book stores, online web-stores, and conventions nationwide. Publisher makes no guarantees of sales quantities or revenues earned by the comic book.

The Comic will be printed in black and white, to be solicited, printed, and released in stores on a date set by Publisher, agreed upon by Creator.

Publisher agrees to advertise the comic book on many standard comic book industry fan websites and in the primary industry Distributor's catalog, PREVIEWS. Publisher will arrange for interviews with website column writers and editors.

Publisher will arrange to acquire space at comic industry fan conventions and trade shows, and acquire pricing information. Publisher and Creator agree to split the cost of all convention expenses 50/50. Publisher and Creator both agree to attend at least three major fan conventions, with an attendance of over 20,000 people, during the term of the agreement.

Creator agrees to produce pages of the Comic at a rate sufficient to meet the deadlines agreed upon with the Publisher. Creator understands that timely production of the Comic and meeting deadlines is a vital part of the success of the Comic.

Creator agrees to pay for all supplies necessary in the creation of the Comic, such as paper, pencils, ink pens, and computer hardware. Creator and Publisher agree that Creator is allowing one-time usage of the art created, and that all future printings of the art, other than for promotional or review purposes, must be renegotiated once the term expires. Creator maintains ownership of all "original art", defined as the physical artwork that is later transferred to digital files, and is free to sell the art at whatever price the Creator desires.

During the term, Publisher may use the Creator's art in any media format, for promotional purposes.

Payment

Publisher and Creator agree to share the net profits of all revenues generated by The Comic 50/50. Net Profits shall be defined as all moneys earned minus the expense of printing, online and print advertising, shipping, distribution fees, and website hosting fees. Costs not deducted from Net Profits will be traveling expenses, convention expenses or Creator expenses for shipping artwork to Publisher.

It is understood that the first payment received by the distributor will be thirty days after the debut of the Comic in stores. Publisher agrees to pay Creator any moneys owed from the first distributor check within two weeks of receiving that first payment from the Distributor.

All following distributor payments shall be accrued by Publisher, and paid at the end of every quarter of each year following, as shall all sales from online stores.

Publisher will provide Creator with an itemized list of expenses and income from the Comic, and upon the Creator's request, will provide copies of invoices and receipts associated with the itemized list.

Convention revenues from the sales of the Comic will be shared 50/50 between Creator and Publisher, unless otherwise agreed to. From time to time, distribution of money from convention sales may be handled on a special case basis. The Creator will retain all money from the sale of original art or commissioned sketches produced at conventions.

Ownership

Publisher and Creator agree to share the ownership rights of the Comic, and all associated characters and trademarks from the Comic, 75/25. The Publisher, who is the party who conceived of the Comic, will own 75% of ownership rights, and the Creator shall own 25%. In the event of merchandising of the Comic's associated trademarks, all distribution of moneys shall be calculated based on the 75/25 ratio. Ownership rights shall remain split at this ratio indefinitely, notwithstanding any other clause in this agreement related to limited terms.

Publisher has the authority to sell the rights of the Comic to another party, for any category of media, be it comic books, film, television, video games, cell phone downloads, or any other medium, without consultation from the Creator, but all income from the sale of such rights shall be shared based upon the 75/25 ratio. The Creator, of course, still retains the ownership of all artwork created for the Comic, and the use of said art, must be negotiated on a case-by-case basis.

Termination

This agreement will automatically expire two years from the date of execution, unless an extension is negotiated. In the event that either party fails to meet the obligations set forth in the agreement, the opposing party may notify he or she, in writing, of a Breach of Contract. The accused party shall have five business days to rectify the matter. In the event that either party is determined to be in breach after the five day window, this agreement is null and void.

If the Creator is the party in breach, Creator may make no claims of ownership of the Comic, and associated trademarks. Ownership rights shall revert to the publisher 100%.

If the Publisher is the party in breach, Publisher must cease use of all art produced by Creator. Publisher retains 75% ownership of the comic, but the other 25% will remain with Artist, even if the Comic has not yet been completed in full.

In the event of a dispute between the two parties that cannot be settled out of court, both parties agree that the matter shall be settled by arbitration to be administered by a single arbitrator of the American Arbitration Association, under its Commercial Arbitration Rules. The judgment of the arbitrator may be entered in any court having jurisdiction thereof. The place of such arbitration shall be within the County of _____, State of _____. Furthermore, the arbitrator shall award the prevailing party the costs of arbitration, including but not limited to reasonable attorneys' fees, expert witness fees, accounting fees and costs.

INVOICING

Invoicing, or "billing," is arguably the most important aspect of any business, because without it, you can't get paid. I discussed invoicing distributors in the first chapter. However, it's just as important for you and your team members to invoice each other.

Early on, it may not seem like a necessity, but as the months pass, there's no way to remember all of those numbers in your head. Even if the creator is not charging the publisher an up-front cost, accounting is imperative to a well run operation.

For instance, let's say that our friends Caitlin and Sean, who agreed upon splitting the proceeds of *Ninja Pants: The Domination* by fifty-fifty, actually did quite well with their publication. After all costs, they were left with $2,000 profit, and a couple thousand books left in inventory to sell. Originally, each person gets $1,000 a piece—easy enough. Now skip ahead a year. Hundreds more have sold through the distributor, but there have also been some returned copies due to damages during shipping. On top of that, Sean has started an online store, and sold another couple hundred copies online, at full retail price. Now add to that copies sold at conventions—conventions that cost money to attend...

Do you understand why meticulous accounting is important?

I'm currently addressing accounting for the purposes of the creator/publisher relationship; I'm not even talking about taxes. To ensure that you are able to write off as much as possible against your income, and that you can show the IRS that you are not hiding money away, accounting is even more important.

Don't be intimidated, though. It's all just simple math. There are a number of inexpensive accounting programs for both PC and Mac that you can use to keep track of everything. If you can't afford that, there's always the good ol' spiral bound notebook.

Don't forget, you can deduct every expense you incur for your publishing from your book's income at tax time. That's when you start to enjoy the beauty of having your own small business. I highly recommend learning more about the subject, but warn you, once you start, you probably won't be able to stop. The U.S. Tax Code, specifically, is written so much more in favor of business owners than it is for employees that it will shock you.

As I've said before, the standard turnaround time for paying an invoice is within thirty days. You will most likely have a different arrangement if you are sharing profits of sales, but as long as it's documented in your contract, that's okay.

ROYALTY REPORTING

This is the not-so-fun aspect of the administrative side of publishing, but as long as you stay organized, it shouldn't be a big deal. In contrast, receiving royalty checks is pretty fun.

The most common standard for reporting royalties is to pay on a quarterly basis, every three months. Along with a check to your team members, you should also provide a report of what has sold, and how much money has been made or lost. If your operation is fairly simple, you may choose to do monthly reporting.

It's also a good idea to divide them up into categories, such as "direct market, book market, online sales, and convention sales." Please see an example of a basic royalty report in the Appendix.

REPUTATION: YEARS TO BUILD, SECONDS TO SHATTER

One could probably write an entire book on this subject. Hell, I'm sure someone has, but I feel compelled to stress your responsibility as a publisher to maintain integrity. You will have a lot of people putting a lot of sweat and blood into every comic book you produce, and it is important that your word means something.

When someone does not hold up his/her end of the bargain, it is bad for the entire comic book industry. Know that you will be entering this business only a short amount of time after dozens of artists and creators were unscrupulously burned by a few major publishers no longer around today. I won't name names, but they know who they are, and they have made publishing comics harder on everyone.

I would love to see a new generation of publishers who care about the comic book industry enough to maintain a sense of honor within it, maybe take a cue from all of those superhero books they read growing up.

What happens all too often in comics is that people go into the business with rose-colored glasses. Despite the research that tells them that they probably won't make any money publishing a small press comic book no one's heard of before, they convince themselves that their idea will sell better than "all those other wannabes." Then the orders come in and they're a quarter of what was expected. Suddenly, the publisher can't pay a team member what s/he promised to pay, and so s/he starts to tell little white lies. Or worse: when creators call or email, he publisher doesn't even respond to them.

This is why it is so important—to all parties—to have a contract, and to only promise what you can afford to pay in the worst-case scenario. If everything goes well, all the better, but you will sleep better at night knowing you haven't bitten off more than you can chew.

If a publisher does not heed this advice, and makes a mistake, the best thing to do is suck it up, grow some juevos, and tell your team the truth: you screwed up. See if you can renegotiate a deal with them to pay them less based on your orders. Most people will understand and have sympathy. Some will insist on the full amount, which you will just have to pay off slowly. Everyone may be upset. They may scream at you, or berate you in emails—and you may well deserve it. The most important thing, though, is to pay them. Live up to your end of the bargain. If it takes you a year to pay them back, when all is said and done, they will at least respect you.

I have made mistakes myself. I've had to pay people late, and they've not been happy about it. Their biggest concern deep down is that they will not be paid at all, because they've been screwed by people before. No matter what they said at the time, and no matter what they thought of me, I friggin' paid them off.

The reputation I've built over the years has helped me. People who know me well will vouch for me, and treat me just as well as I treat them. Simple concept, isn't it? I had one run-in with a group of people who, it turned out, had been lying to artists and writers, and making a ton of promises they couldn't possibly keep. When confronted, they wouldn't listen to my concerns, so I had to pull away from them. Making the situation worse, they were blaming their problems on me. I could not let this ruin my reputation, and had to fight back.

Fortunately, my current reputation was stronger than theirs and, with a few exceptions, most observers believed me. The whole situation bothered me, but I just moved on. You know what? Eventually, the ones who hated me the absolute most—my former partners' most loyal team members— eventually came back over a year later and let me know they were sorry they ever doubted me. They eventually saw through the lies. Honesty and integrity always win out in the end—and it helps to have a solid reputation already in place.

I'm not really a spiritual person, so I don't believe in karma, but have no doubt: "what goes around, comes around" is a simple game of odds. I have worked for ten years in the business and slowly developed a very solid reputation. Yet if I were to bail out on just a few people, it could tarnish my name for the next thirty years.

Plus, following through on your word is just the right thing to do.

Beau Smith is an industry veteran who's been around for years. He was instrumental in the early days of Image Comics as the head of marketing, and he's written too many comics and video games to count. I'll never forget Beau because he treated me with respect from the moment I met him, when I was only 18. He said one of the best pieces of advice that everyone should take to heart: "In this business, you never know who your boss will be tomorrow."

Moral of the story? Treat everyone well. I've had the

fortune of being treated well by people for the most part, but I've also been burned by a lot too, and make no mistake, more than a few of them tried to get on my good side later. When I was young and new, they treated upstarts like me as if we were dogshit, but when they want me to come to their convention or publish their book, do you think I will? Hell no!

Maybe that makes me the lesser person, but I say screw those people. There are too many good people out there to waste your time with 'em.

I'm not saying you should expect special treatment if you're new to the biz. If Devil's Due is at a convention, having a serious problem with booth set-up, and you're simultaneously in Artist Alley with a problem, they're probably going to take care of us first. It's just the way it is, but they should treat you with respect. And guess what? If Todd McFarlane or Stan Lee need attention, they're going to get it way before Devil's Due does. So understand the business side of things, but you don't have to accept being treated like crap.

WHERE THE HECK DO I FIND THESE PEOPLE?

When the Godfathers of the Golden Age comic book industry were ushering in a new era of four-color heroes, everyone worked from the same studio. The big comic book publishers were almost all based in New York. Guys like Stan Lee, Julie Schwartz, Jack Kirby, and Steve Ditko worked from offices that had "bullpens" where the artists and writers interacted face to face.

Then came the dawn of FedEx, and overnight delivery services. Suddenly, artists could work from home, sending their pages in once or twice a month, and the publisher no longer had to assume the risk of hiring on so many full time employees. That was the early '70s, and it stayed that way until, yes, that gift from God known as high speed internet access!

Man, I swore I wouldn't date myself, because I want this book to help the modern self-publisher, but it's so hard to write about these topics without contemplating just how quickly things have changed in less than a decade. It blows my mind… and also fills me with anticipation for how quickly they will continue to change.

The new skool creators and publishers have so many

great tools at their disposal that didn't exist a few blinks ago.

Back in the day, if you wanted to find others to collaborate on a comic book project, you were relegated to asking your other friends in art class, or meeting someone at the local comic shop. If you were very serious, you would travel to one of the big conventions, and try to meet as many creators as possible.

Comics Buyer's Guide, now a monthly magazine, was a weekly newspaper that many people placed classified ads in, seeking talent. Still, that took weeks, and then you had to wait for photocopies of art samples to arrive in the mail.

Today? Man, today you can find the most amazing talent in a matter of seconds. There is *no* reason anyone should have to publish a comic book of unprofessional quality. Take the time to seek out talent *before* you begin, and it will save you months of struggling down the line.

The old ways still work, but try sniffing around on the web's many artist communities and message boards to see what you can find. Two great websites I recommend are Deviant Art (deviantart.com) and Digital Webbing (digital-webbing.com).

IT ALL COMES DOWN TO COMMUNICATION

In the ideal situation, no one ever needs to bust out an old contract for a dispute. Hopefully it's never needed. If there ever is any confusion between you and your team members, though, you'll sure be glad that you took the time to write a detailed agreement. This is all part of clear communication.

The biggest wastes of time and effort, the biggest feuds in the history of the world, and the biggest expenses for companies come from poor communication. No one sets out to communicate poorly, but few people always make an effort to communicate well. It's in human nature to make certain assumptions, and it's those assumptions that bite you in the ass later.

As time goes on, and you make more deals, problems will arise that neither party anticipated. There's just no way around it. All you can do is handle the situation to the best of your ability—and make sure, if something particularly bad happens, to include a new clause in any future contracts expressly to prevent repeating the ordeal.

Having these agreements in place will allow you to move on to the fun part of publishing – creating a comic book! You'll be able to sleep better at night knowing that you are handling things like the pros, and that the journey you are about to go through with your team members should be one of cooperation, and few, if any misunderstandings.

All right, ready? Time for the next stage: Marketing and Production. You can have the best comic book in the world, but if you don't know how to market it, and no one hears about it, you'll never sell enough to sustain yourself. Even more important, if you don't know how to handle the transition of your artwork and computer files from your home computer to the printer, you won't be able to deliver on time.

Printing and Marketing

INTRODUCTION

In the previous chapters I covered the territories of setting
up your self-publishing infrastructure and signing your
creative team. With those two elements in place, the creation of your book is underway. Creating the comic is only
half the battle, though. Now you have the assignment of
making sure everyone knows about it, and making sure it gets
into the stores on time. Hence the subjects of this chapter,
MARKETING (getting the word out about your comic or
manga) and **PRODUCTION** (getting it from the creators to
the printer to the stores).

THE HOOK

It all starts with the "hook." If you don't have a hook, you don't have anything to market. The hook is what makes your concept stand out from all of the others. Too often people try to explain every detail about their character or story, and lose the reader's interest. You only have a split second to grab someone's attention before they move on to another comic, so make that second count.

For example, if you told someone you were writing a 100-page graphic novel about Santa Claus, most people are going to stare at you and walk away. But if you have a hook, for instance, "*Santa Claus Vs. the Four Horsemen of the Apocalypse in 2215,*" you might pique their interest. *I'd* read that story, but maybe that's not the best example.

Another example is a concept I'm working on called *Mercy Sparx*. This started as an excuse for me to draw what I enjoy drawing – punk-influenced imagery like cute girls in the rock and hip hop scenes, cartoony devil girls, urban settings, etc. There are a lot of books like this, and there are countless cartoony devil-girls found in both comics and music. My hook: *Mercy Sparx is a devil girl secretly hired by Heaven to hunt down angels who've abandoned their duties.* Sure, there's a lot more to it than that, but I can tell you the overall concept in one sentence, and hopefully pique your interest in the process.

All of the marketing can then revolve around the hook.

THE PLANNING STARTS **NOW**

The hardest thing for people to grasp is usually just how far in advance your promotion needs to start. Solicitations (covered previously) are due to the distributors no less than four months before your book debuts, and if you're selling to the bookstores, it's more like eight months.

That means at minimum, you need to have the cover art, and any other imagery you want to accompany your advertising, underway about a month before that. It sounds like a long time, doesn't it? Then you need to take into consideration that there has been more competition than ever in the recent year, and it's not going to stop.

The last thing you want to do is to rush your book into the distributor catalogs and into the stores without having planned out a year's worth of promotion first. More and more these days I'm developing the philosophy that no promotion plan is too extensive. Take hit sellers like *MegaTokyo*. This was an online strip forever before finally being released as a manga digest graphic novel. That time on the web helped it earn a following of thousands of people, and that same audience translated into sales once the title jumped from cyberspace to bookshelves. More recently, Dark Horse just pulled off the same phenomenon with *Penny Arcade*, which as of press time reportedly has sold 30,000 copies.

My saying this about marketing comes from experience. I confess, I haven't always practiced what I preach. Even after years in business, and after learning all of this, sometimes things get so hectic at the office that we allow a book to go through without marketing it as far in advance as we should. That's very rare, though! Sometimes one can only learn from experience, so even when someone is telling you that it would be a good idea to do x, y and z, it's not the same as learning it for yourself.

So to you I say, learn from my mistakes! Don't wait until you've made this mistake yourself.

I put long-term marketing strategies in the same category as going to the gym, eating healthy, and not smoking. It's just really damn hard to do, even though you know it's the right thing to do. People do things that are detrimental to their health because doing the right thing is more painful. It's events like having a heart attack that make it more painful in your mind not to eat like crap. Well, only after your book's sales come in at zilch do you kick yourself for not doing all the marketing that you should have done.

Of course, the Catch-22 is, you might promote the hell out of your book, and it still might not sell very well, the same way you might eat all of your vegetables every day, but get hit by a bus. Playing the odds, I'd say we're all safer off doing the right thing.

"But Blaylock, I don't have any friggin' money to spend on marketing!" you may be thinking. Sure, having some money is a necessity. You have to have, or be acquiring some money, otherwise self-publishing might be out of your realm of possibility, but stretching those funds might seem harder than it actually is. I understand where you're coming from, though, and will do my best to explain how to stretch that penny so far it turns into copper wire.

The three major categories of marketing are:

BREAK IT DOWN, YO

PRINT
ONLINE
FACE TO FACE

And your two completely different target markets are:
READERS
RETAILERS

PRINT MARKETING
Traditional Print Advertising

Advertising in print is no doubt one of the most expensive means of marketing. It's imperative that you advertise a **FULL PAGE** in the distributor catalog when introducing your title to the world. That's the easy one. You need to seriously consider where else, if anywhere, to spend your other print advertising dollars, as well as arrange for any opportunities to trade (or "swap") ads with other publications.

Say for instance that you somehow earn the funds to advertise in a major magazine publication like *Maxim* or *Spin* (imagination here, people) and you want to get a full page ad. Will this expensive advertisement actually produce sales?

Would it really do any good? How many outlets are there for those millions of people to go buy your comic book? The same goes for spending big money to advertise locally in newspapers and weekly street publications. If you only have four comic shops in your city, and you're not in the major bookstore chains with a graphic novel yet, it doesn't make sense to spend any cash. Lastly, it's likely that over 90% of the people reading those publications are not in your **TARGET MARKET**. Target Market is exactly what it sounds like: your potential "targets," or customers most likely to buy your comic or manga.

For instance, you're going to have a lot stronger chance of hitting your target market by advertising in a comic convention program, or sending postcards to a hundred major comic book shops than you are running an ad in, say, *TV Guide*.

The cardinal rule for print advertising—for any advertising—is that repetition counts. It is far more effective to buy six months' worth of quarter-page ads in a publication, running an ad each month, or multiple ads throughout the book, than it is to blow everything on one or two full-page ads that are gone in the blink of an eye.

All of this talk about aiming for your target market may seem obvious, but I see the same mistakes made over and over again. I think that when people are knee-deep in their project, they just lose sight of the big picture sometimes. It's hard not to when you're so close to it.

I emphasize again that the one place you must use a full page of advertising is when promoting your first issue in the distributor catalog; there are so many comic books shipping each month, it is your only chance to be noticed. If you can't do it, don't bother trying to self-publish comics through the Direct Market. The repetition factor comes into play when you've been in the catalog multiple times.

Flyers, Postcards, and Inserts

Bands do it, local businesses do it, and you can too. The good old fashioned flyer is an effective way to get your idea across to many people in a short amount of time. One might be tempted to head to the local copy center to print up a few hundred leaflets, but before you do, check online for other alternatives.

Companies such as Club Flyers and PS Prints offer as many as 5,000 full color postcards for under $200. Let me tell you, that's a lot of postcards. These are perfect to send to comic book shops so retailers can hand them out to customers, or to leave on the "free tables" at major conventions. Remember to apply the same principal as discussed above regarding your target market. Don't waste your postcards by handing them out at Burger King, or anywhere that has nothing to do with comic books.

Your distributor should offer marketing programs in which they will include inserts into catalogs or newsletters sent to retailers, although these may be a little pricy. It all depends on your budget. Some argue that it's actually more effective to mail batches of flyers or cards directly to the retailers yourself.

As always, you only have so many hours in the day, so make sure that whatever you're doing is as effective as possible. Keep your message simple. Don't flood the flyer with too much text. I suggest one side of the flyer contain one powerful image, your logo, and one short catch phrase, to grab the viewer's interest. Keep all of the detailed information on the other side.

Things that you should include on the back of the flyer include: the distributor order code for your title (every comic book has one); your website, for anyone who wants more information; the Comic Shop Locator phone number (1-888-COMIC-BOOK) and a short synopsis of what the book is about. Emphasis on *short*. This is not a summary of your entire issue—rather it is the "hook."

Timing

Timing is everything, so much so that I'm going to discuss it at the end of each of the three major marketing categories. Since comic book solicitations run in the comic shop catalogs two months before the book is scheduled to hit the shelves, you need to have your print ads out before that. I'd recommend advertising three or four months before the books hit the catalogs, and continue to advertise until one month after the catalog hits.

That month after the catalogs hit the stands is when customers are giving their order requests to retailers, and when you push them into that all important, make-or-break decision, "Yeah, I'll give this book a shot." That's it. Everything you're doing, all of the months and months of preparation and hundreds to thousands of dollars you're spending revolve around getting the customer to say "I'll check it out."

I don't want to mislead you into thinking that this is the only marketing you'll do. Marketing never stops, at least if you're releasing more than one issue or volume. This is just how you put yourself on the map.

ONLINE MARKETING

Ahh, online marketing, the savior of the financially limited. There will come a day when online marketing is more valuable than television and print combined, and some would say that day has already arrived. Fortunately, the costs to do so have not caught up with their effectiveness. There are a plethora (that's fancy for "buttload") of free and low cost marketing opportunities online that hit your ultimate target markets.

The Website

The most obvious, and one of the most important tools for online marketing is your website. This is the nucleus that all of your other online marketing efforts revolve around. You want to draw the audience to your site to find out all about your comic. As surprising as this may sound to some, I don't think the traditional website is going to remain as important as it has been, if they don't disappear altogether. Online Networking Portals have already started to take over the personal website, and are becoming more important to businesses. I'll stop trying to predict the future, though, because I'm sure whatever dominates next hasn't even been created yet.

So, back to your website:

There are a number of companies that offer simple website software packages that can be accessed completely online. I prefer TypePad for my personal website (because I'm pretty html-ignorant), but for Devil's Due our webmaster uses something much more complex. Take a couple of hours and search online for what's out there.

We all know that websites can be as complex as you want them to be, but they all need to contain a few key elements to effectively spread the word about your product.

First, it needs to be easy to navigate, and should be updated regularly with news items and updates. This may be in the form of a "behind the scenes" blog, regular postings of work in progress, or both. My company's website, DevilsDue. net, is updated multiple times a week, although it gets tough to keep my personal site updated. Try to structure in time to update at least once a week. That's what keeps people coming back to your site.

Once you get them to your site, you really want viewers to hang around for a while. A great way to do this is by building a message board community. Message boards, or Forums, are just a place for everyone to post their comments publicly. There are a number of free message board services you can sign up for, while maintaining a professional look.

You want to create as much "viral" marketing material as you can, called so because once it's out of your hands it spreads like a virus. These can be in the form of screen wallpaper images, web-banners that link back to your website, message board avatars, or instant message icons. Anyone with basic graphic design abilities and a copy of Adobe Photoshop or Illlustrator can make these in a short amount of time. As long as the masses think they look cool, you'll start to see them pop up on their own forum posts, MySpace pages, and websites.

Freebies

The immediate, and easiest advertising is simply message board posting. There are a number of online forums that are free to register for, and are flooded by comic and manga readers. There is so much out there that your challenge is not going to be finding them, but rather determining which ones to weed out, because you only have so many hours in the day.

There's no message board that I know of where people go to read posts from random individuals pitching their comic ideas to readers, but websites like Newsarama and Broken

Frontier have active message board communities that discuss everything from the articles posted on these sites, to their thoughts on—well, their thoughts on just about every damn thing in the world. What you need to do is get active on these boards. See, every time you post, you have an opportunity to direct someone to your website. Yeah, that's right, you have to have a website.

Every message board forum allows you to attach a "signature," a brief piece of text and a web-link of your choice, and in most cases, a small image. Every time you post a comment, you're advertising—even if it's just to join an argument about whether or not Storm Shadow from *G.I. Joe* or the Shredder from *Teenage Mutant Ninja Turtles* would win in a fight.

Now, I am not recommending that you go on every single thread in every single forum and tell everyone that you are publishing a comic book. Keep your post subjects related to the subject of discussion, unless you are in a specific thread about self-promotion.

YourSpace: Online Networking Portals

If you haven't heard of, or if you're not on MySpace, there's a good chance you're over thirty years old. MySpace, Friendster, Facebook—these are websites that allow you to customize your own page, photo albums, blogs and calendars, and link them with other people all over the world. I can't help but almost laugh while I'm typing this explanation, because in a few short years, these portals will be as commonplace as terminology like "website" or "internet," and the fact that I'm trying to explain them right now will be amusing in and of itself.

I already have friends who don't even bother to call or email people about parties or events anymore. Posting it on

MySpace is considered enough of an effort.

I'm sure new portals will pop up all over the place, but currently MySpace is the only one I'd put any serious effort into. This is a great way to spread the word about your comic. The cool thing is, you can make a profile for one of your characters, as if the character was real, and had a page of his/her own. I'd recommend having one based on your character, or tied into some major aspect of your book—like a fictitious city—and then having one about the real you. Yes, I have a MySpace page, and you can go there and read my blog and see pictures of me doing stupid things like playing with toy ninjas or pretending to sing karaoke.

ONPs can be used in a very similar way as your traditional website by including links to web banners, wallpapers and icons. They are an even better way to network with fellow comic and manga creators. I recently spent a couple of weeks attempting to contact an artist who Devil's Due wanted to work with for an upcoming project, and got ahold of him on MySpace in one day.

Press Releases

So your website is ready to go, your ONP is set up, and you have a list of forums to start regularly posting on. It's time to let the world know about your comic book. The way to do this is with the traditional press release. A simple, one page announcement that explains the who, what, when, where, and why about your new creation. Who's publishing and creating it, what is it about, when is it debuting, where can people find it, and why should they care?

Everyone has seen press releases, but not everyone has written them. There are a few key rules for press releases, but they're very simple. The problem I see with most bad PRs is that the writer overcomplicates them. I've included a sample press release with notes in the back of this issue to help explain how to make yours the most effective.

If anyone's intimidated about writing one, don't be. I actually credit learning everything I needed to know about press releases to my 8th grade journalism teacher.

You can easily email these PRs to the major comic book news websites, magazine editors, and comic bookstores. You can send them anywhere you want, including the local press. Getting an article in your hometown newspaper doesn't usually translate to many sales, but it's nice to show the folks at home, and gives Grandma something to brag about.

Paid Banner Ads

There's so much you can do for free online that it's hard to swallow spending money, but it's worth doing so in some places. For example, websites like Newsarama.com, Comic-BookResources.com, ICV2.com, BrokenFrontier.com, and many more have huge followings of avid comic book readers. Some are strictly comic book news sites, while others cover information about toys, cartoons and video games too.

Some of these sites get as many as 50,000 visitors a day, which is probably a heck of a lot more than your own website's going to get. Posting a banner ad on there for a few months can greatly increase your exposure for a nominal fee, and start to burn the image of your comic into the readers' minds.

Interviews

Now that word of your press release has spread all over the planet, everyone will be banging down your door for an interview! Okay, maybe you won't be that lucky, but hopefully your book interests some comic journalists enough to request a Q&A. If not, though, don't be afraid to contact them and ask. Don't be pushy, and don't take offense if they just aren't interested. You're new to the game, and it may just take a while.

It's no guarantee, but throwing a few bucks towards some advertising never hurts when you want a website to cover your story.

Previews

As you start to receive completed images from your comic book, they always make for good teaser material to show readers. Previews can be fully colored, lettered pages, or just sketches of characters. You have to decide the best way to show off your product, and get everyone interested. If you have interviews lined up, the reporter will usually request images from you. You can also send out previews to sites in the same manner that you send the press releases, and post them on your website or ONP.

Devil's Due posts five page previews of every book that we have coming out each week. Not only does it get people excited, but it gives them a reason to revisit the site on a regular basis. Each time they visit our website, they may see something new that peaks their interest that they otherwise may have glossed over.

While it's not the preferred method, there's nothing wrong with posting your own Q&A on your website, if it takes you awhile to get any interest. You may also send preview copies of your entire comic to online reviewers. Good reviews can make all the difference, as well as lead to more press.

Email Newsletters

You need to be careful that you don't violate any spam laws, or irritate fans with too many messages, but using email newsletters is a great way to inform thousands of people about your product with but a click of the mouse. I recommend using a service offered online, such as Constant Contact, that allows you to craft clear, easy to read HTML emails, so it's basically like you're sending a small web page to your customers.

Services like this automatically delete invalid emails, people who wish to unsubscribe, and duplicate entries, as well as allow you to easily add names to your list. If you keep an updated email list, this makes every single "face to face" promotional event that you do a chance to build your database.

Timing

Since online marketing is so inexpensive, it's never too early to start. I would actually encourage you to have your entire online marketing plan ready to go before you even put pencil to paper. That means knowing specifically where you're going to advertise, what your website will entail, and purchasing any necessary software.

The thing to remember is that, unless you're already an established professional artist or writer, no one has ever heard of you. No one has heard of your comic book, so it doesn't pay to be mysterious. If you're afraid to show people glimpses of your project, afraid you'll spoil the surprise, no one is going to hear about it, and therefore no one will buy it, and there won't be anyone to enjoy the surprise. Start showing sketches and conceptual images from your project as soon as possible. Get people talking.

You don't have to tell them everything, but you need to

make sure that by the time your book comes out, thousands of people have had the chance to hear about it. Like I said earlier, don't hesitate to promote your book for an entire year before it actually debuts.

FACE TO FACE MARKETING

Face to face is probably the hardest way to market your product, but it never hurts to get out there and meet the people who are actually reading your book. In the next chapter we'll cover exhibiting at conventions, which is as face to face as you can get.

There are also store signings. Talk to your local stores, or stores near conventions you may be attending about going to their shops and drawing sketches for fans or signing books. Try to make sure you're going to a good store first, so you don't waste a lot of extra time and effort, but also don't have unrealistic expectations. Unless you are *the* hot shit, you're not going to pack a store with customers. Take advantage of this, though, to issue another press release to the online websites, collect email addresses from the fans you meet, and above all, be nice.

Other than conventions and store signings, you need to think outside of the box for this style of marketing. Perhaps you target the local movie theatre chains and hand out flyers during a weekend that a major comic-book inspired movie debuts, and inform the local press. Maybe you cooperate with a local DJ to host an event where imagery from your comics is displayed. Sometimes you might just want to do this for fun, regardless of the sales potential it translates into, but always keep that in mind so you don't burn yourself out.

Timing

Timing your face to face appearances isn't much different than other marketing efforts, with the exception that you need to do just as much of it after your book debuts. The up side is that you have a chance to sell copies and recoup some, if not all, of your money.

Just like solicitations for catalogs, and ad deadlines for print publications, you need to reserve your trade show appearances in advance. The more popular the show or event, the more likely it is you will need to book early.

READERS

Up until now, this has most likely been you. You probably buy your comic books every Wednesday at the local shop, or peruse the bookshelves at Borders looking for the latest manga offerings. Either way, you know your habits, now it's time to really think about them.

How do you go about choosing your comic book or manga purchases? What makes you decide to pick up a book that is not released by the major publishers? What is your age, race, and sex? Are you the same demographic as the majority of other comic book readers, or are your habits or characteristics different than most? If you have very eclectic tastes, and, in the eyes of others, you know that you just like "weird" stuff, you need to make sure your product will not be too far from the center to find an audience.

I still struggle with this problem even today. I've always been too weird for the normal people, and too normal for the weirdos. You just have to know your niche, and know what reactions to expect to your concept. If you're not in the majority, ask other readers a few key questions about why they buy certain comic books, and if they only rarely buy small press / independent comics, ask them what triggers that decision.

Although I don't have any concrete data to give you specifics, the average comic bookstore customer is male, Caucasian, and 25 to 40 years old. I know, I know, 18 to 35 is a much more popular statistic used, but I don't believe it. I think that's outdated, and our closed off comic shop audience is getting older. That's why, even though I don't particularly enjoy a lot of manga, I love the whole phenomenon of it, because it has brought the youth back into this medium, and even better, a healthy ratio of female and male readers.

Most comic shop customers have "Pull Boxes" reserved at their local store. Susan Bishop, head of Devil's Due's marketing, wrote a great explanation of the Pull Box recently, displayed at the end of the section.

Pull boxes are convenient for customers, but they're a double edged sword. Me, I'm a rack browser, I like to peruse the shelves for the latest releases and pull a handful of comics down. I request some of the harder to find indy comics, but the pull box sort of ruins the experience for me. Many people only buy what's in their pull box, though, and hardly look around. So if you didn't capture their attention in Previews or online, you may already be out of luck. That's why marketing ahead of time is so important.

The internet is a great way to get people talking about a book, but I also believe the amount of readers who go online to receive comic book news every day is a much smaller percentage than those who *do* receive their info that way think. It's easy to lose sight of this when you're knee deep in publishing. All of the *real* sales happen when you get a word of mouth buzz. The comic shop is like a barber-shop for all of our fellow comic geeks; people like to hang out and talk, and the people who've read the gossip online love to spread the word when they meet with their shop owners and peers.

The bookstore customer is much different, though, due to the mainstream accessibility of major book chains, and the popularization of manga through weekday anime cartoons. There's not so much of a "secret club" mentality. It's much more casual, as customers simply browse the shelves looking for the latest releases. Since most of the bookstore offerings are graphic novels too, serialized books don't usually come out every single month like the thinner comic books.

Don't get me wrong, there is a huge manga following of very, very, very passionate fans to rival the most die-hard Clark Kent fanatic or Jedi in training, but the availability of these stores has helped them to become more mainstream. When I was in high school you could repel an entire army of girls with a comic book (it was like a magic trick!) and these days guys actually *meet* girls that way. My how times have changed.

Part of this is also thanks to much larger cultural changes. We're a much more cartoon-friendly society than we were twenty years ago, and that makes comics less "geeky." Or it makes being a "geek" cooler. That's one you can argue for a week. My Dad, for instance, refuses to watch any cartoons, no matter how damn funny they may be. He just can't get past the mentality that they're for kids. Me? Hell, I hardly watch anything *except* cartoons, whether it's *Family Guy* (available as a comic book from Devil's Due!), Adult Swim, *South Park, The Simpsons*… as long as it's not *Drawn Together*. I stay clear of that one.

My point is that while there are many more challenges facing comic books than ever before, there is more opportunity than ever as well. I can't guarantee that comic shops or bookstores will be your best path to choose, but you need to consider both in your plan, and consider various formats that make the most sense for whatever you choose to do. If you never go to the major bookstores, take an evening and check some out. Are you a manga fan who only shops at Borders? Head down to the nearest comic shops and see what they have to offer, because they may have the potential to be a valuable part of your sales.

THE ART OF THE PULL BOX

A Pull Box (aka Pull & Hold Service, Club Membership, Comic Book Subscription Service) is a helpful service most comic shops offer their customers. As a reader, you provide a list of comics that you want–monthly titles, special orders, whatever you need–and the shop pulls those titles aside for you every week, so you don't miss a single issue. Plus, many shops offer a discount for keeping a pull box!

Your comic shop (and even comic fans) uses *Previews Magazine*, a monthly catalog of comicky goodness listing all of the comics that will be out two months later, so you know what to order for your own pull box. Only comic shops can order directly from *Previews*, but your shop should stock *Previews*, or have a copy available to look through. *Previews* comes out the last Wednesday of every month.

PRODUCTION

So you've created and marketed the heck out of your comic book. Now it's time to send it off to the printer. It's not that complicated, but it's not magic either. This is the **PRODUCTION** process. As long as you stay organized, and keep an open line of communication with your printer and distributor, everything should go smoothly.

TURNAROUND

You need to budget in about five weeks from the time your comic book files leave your hands, until the printed copies hit the stands. Discuss this with your printer and distributor to be sure, but it's a safe estimate. Many new publishers don't realize quite how long the production side takes, so don't get caught by surprise. If you have opted to use an overseas printer, know that it will take much longer to receive your books, because they have to come over on the "slow boat."

Your orders may not arrive from distributors until four weeks before the books are expected to be in stores, but don't wait for them. Go ahead and make arrangements with your printer anyway, so that they can be ready to run the presses at the word "go."

SET UP CHARGES: BOOK ASSEMBLY

There are a number of ways to send your finished comic book computer files into the printer. The less finished they are, though, the more it may cost you, or the longer it may take to print your book. If you don't have anything except original artwork and hand lettering, for instance, the printer will have to scan all of your pages, resize them, and assemble them in the computer for print, and they're going to charge you for that.

Hopefully you can at least send them individual files of each page burnt onto a CD, so that they only have to assemble them, and send them to the press.

At Devil's Due we try to deliver files ready to send straight to the printer. We assemble all of the individual lettered art files in a program like Adobe InDesign, and from there generate a PDF. This is the kind of file that today's digital printing presses all read. If you don't send the printer an assembled PDF, they're probably going to be making one themselves.

Some printers allow you to upload your files via the internet, which saves an extra day and an extra FedEx bill, so be sure to ask. Do not attempt this, though, if you do not have high-speed internet access.

No matter how you send your files, you must be sure to send a printer mock. This is a "mock" copy of the finished comic book (not necessarily as nice as the one described earlier for sending to book buyers), but good enough for the printer to see what is supposed to be on each page. This can just be a bunch of copies stapled together, but make sure the mock-up reads just like the book, and that no pages are out of order, including covers.

When the printer has received your materials, they will

send you a printer proof for review. This is your last chance to check for errors in your book. Sometimes the mistakes were yours, but sometimes the printer mixes up files, so be sure to look carefully. They will not print the book until you sign an approval form, and fax it back. In a worst case scenario, you may approve via a PDF that you read onscreen, but that's very risky. If for instance, the files are too low of a resolution, and look pixelated in print, they may still look fine on screen.

Once you sign off: congratulations! Your brand new baby is about to be born!

ORDERS ARE IN!

The first thing to do when your orders arrive is to get your purchase order from the distributor(s). The distributor will provide you with the dates to expect orders to be in. For more info on POs, see issue one. The PO will not only list the amount of total copies ordered, along with the pricing information, but will include a breakdown of various warehouses certain quantities need to be shipped to. Distributors maintain various warehouses in different regions of the country, and this is how they get so many products out everywhere on the same day.

It is important to give this information to your printer, so they know how to divide the print run, and how many copies to ship to each place.

Don't forget to include how many copies you want sent to yourself, and to anyone else who contributed to the comic book. How many do you expect to sell via reorders and at conventions? Did you pre-sell any copies on your webstore?

What we like to do at Devil's Due is have a handful of copies sent via FedEx to our offices, and to various people associated with each particular title, so that we can see them before they arrive in stores. You may choose to let a book hit the stands before you've seen a printed copy, but if so, you're more of a gambler than I am.

The remainder of the copies are either sent via ground delivery service, or in the case of a printer like Quebecor, picked up by the Diamond Distributor trucks at the crack of dawn each Wednesday morning. Whatever books are picked up that Wednesday will hit the stands the following Wednesday.

SETTING YOUR PRINT RUN

Once you know how many copies you need, it's time to set your print run. You should already have some preliminary quotes from your printer, but may have to request additional information if your orders were more or less than you expected.

The lower your print run, the higher the cost per book. A lot of the time spent in the printing process is getting the paper and ink set up on the press. So it's a lot easier to keep the presses running to print 10,000 copies than it is to print five books at 2,000 copies apiece.

This is where you may find yourself getting more books than you need, simply because it doesn't cost much more to print 5,000 copies as it does to print 3,000 copies of a comic. Sometimes it's almost the same price. Be sure to read your quotes carefully so you don't miss out on an opportunity like this.

The last thing to arrange is where you'll be keeping your inventory. Most comic books come shipped in about 200 copies per box, so if you're only holding onto a few hundred copies an issue, it might be no problem to keep them in your house. If you're storing thousands, though, you'll need to make arrangements. Most printers will store your books for a very nominal fee. Then, as you need more, or you need more sent to distributors, they will ship them for you.

QUESTIONS ARE GOOD

Never hesitate to ask your printer or your distributor questions. No one expects you to have all of the answers, and the only dumb questions are the ones not asked.

There is plenty of information about both marketing and production to fill entire books by themselves (and there are many on marketing at your local bookstore), but hopefully this helps get you started. Once your wheels start turning, there's no stopping you. Just don't be afraid to seek out more information, and get out there and learn the best way: from experience.

CHAPTER 4
Hitting the Pavement

C EVER, INC.

BLAY

Hitting the Pavement

INTRODUCTION

So you've followed through on building your infrastructure, signing a creative team, as well as marketing and production, but hopefully you realized one thing: it doesn't stop there!

Unless your only goal was to publish a one-shot comic or manga to fulfill a longtime dream, and now you're content, you're going to need to continue marketing the heck out of your publication. If you published a one-shot title to get noticed by bigger publishers, it's time to start promoting yourself to those companies and their editors. And of course, if you're publishing a series of books there are more issues to produce, and more readers to introduce your comic to, and no time to waste—so let's get rollin'.

This issue focuses on convention promotion. And we're back at the question I posed earlier: *Why are you doing this?* Just as it's important to ask yourself about publishing, it's important to do the same for conventions. Many self-publishers make convention attendance a priority without truly discerning the reasons behind going.

WHAT'S A COMICON?

So what exactly *is* a **COMICON**?

It's hard for me to fathom, but I've been exhibiting at comic book conventions, or comicons, for over a third of my life. Some of you may have only seen them as parodied in film and television. Well, the first thing to get out of the way is that *not everyone wears costumes*. Some are more of a... well, a "nerdfest" than others, but most have expanded to include exhibitors from video game and toy companies, creating an entire "pop culture" experience.

A comicon is usually held in a large hall at a convention center or hotel, and houses displays from various comic book publishers, as well as tables where artists set up examples of their work and draw and sell sketches for the fans. It's one of the only industries that allows fans to meet its "celebrities" face to face, and take a piece of the industry home with them in the form of original art and autographs.

Some of the publishers are there to give away promotional posters and materials, while others sell comics from their entire catalog of titles.

Half of the shows are usually reserved for comic book retailers that set up spaces to sell new and old titles, toys, t-shirts, and pretty much anything else you can imagine.

Conventions typically range from one to three days in length. San Diego's Comicon, the largest of all, is four and one half days. The price of admission for conventions can be anywhere from a few bucks, to over sixty dollars depending on what package an attendee buys, and the size and scope of the show.

MY FIRST CON

My first major convention experience was the 1995 Chicago Comicon. This was two years before Wizard World took over, and a year before I published my first comic book. I had just graduated from high school, and had already encountered my fair share of shysters in the comics biz. Just a couple years earlier everyone was selling comics hand over fist, so many people who had no idea what they were doing jumped into the publishing game. Many of them even made money despite themselves.

I was by no means skilled enough to be professionally published yet, but didn't know that then (or care to wait until I was better), so I jumped at the opportunity to talk to any publisher I could. Most of my interactions with publishers ended with the discovery that they knew even less about the business than I did. Still, I would devour a few more pieces of information in my quest to get my comics out to the world.

Just before the 1995 Chicago Comicon, I had a serious lead on a hot indy publisher. They liked one of my ideas, and wanted to talk. I didn't let my $400 Volkswagen Rabbit stop me, either. If my engine couldn't get me there, I'd do it on faith… or something.

My friend Jerry came along for the ride, and I was so excited I went ahead and left at about 11 pm, figuring I'd drive through the night. It's a miracle we made it alive, because my headlights at the time had what I called the "Ninja Hunter" feature, preferring to illuminate the treetops rather than the road in front of me.

The engine's deficiencies won out over will-power, and we broke down about two hours outside of Cincinnati, in the middle of Indiana. A guy named Harley was nice enough to give us a lift, and call in a tow truck for us. We opted for sleeping in the booth of a 24 hour restaurant rather than a hotel (money doesn't grow on trees, especially when you're 18), after which he was nice enough to pick us up again at 6:00 AM, when he got off of work.

Upon our arrival, we found the auto body shop still closed for the night, so we waited for another three or four hours. Then, finally speaking to a mechanic, I was told, and I quote, "ever'body 'round here drives mostly Fords 'n' Chevys. We don't really work on no foreign cars."

I was at the end of my rope. I somehow convinced him to look at the car, and long story short, we were on the road about 4 or 5 hours later. So, what should have been a 6-hour trip became a 22-hour monumental task, but we made it.

The actual convention part of the trip was cut down to a half day, but I managed to meet with the aforementioned publisher, and a couple weeks later we had a deal! Over the next couple of months I drove to every small convention in a 200 mile radius, printed ashcans, and along with my writing partner, pimped the hell out of that comic.

So why am I telling this story? Because shortly thereafter, I got a phone call from the publisher saying that they weren't going to publish the book, that it really wasn't very good, and not up to par for them. "But you've seen it," I said. "You've known what it looked like for months." The company completely burned us, and that's when I said, "screw it, I'm doing this myself." I made the conscious decision to enter the world of self-publishing.

NETWORKING

Probably the most important effect convention attendance can have for your business is the amount of contacts you make. Relationships developed online or over the telephone pale in comparison to face to face contact. This is where you can meet the hundreds of talented creators that make the industry tick, and even become close friends with many of them.

There's an energy at conventions, a sort of instant bonding that happens between people. It's one of the few times that everyone is linked by a common interest – everyone knows what happens on Wednesdays (for the layman, that's when new comic books hit the shelves)! I've often chatted with friends about how strange it is that you can meet someone at a convention just once, and by the next show you're crashing in their hotel room, and it's like you've known each other forever.

That's the networking that happens naturally, but you also need to make a concerted effort to meet people, pass out your business card to those you chat with, and just get to know people who make comic books for a living. You'll also meet dozens of self-publishers in the same boat as yourself, and you can trade thoughts and ideas, and talk with others who understand where you're coming from.

It used to drive me crazy that I had a hard time getting to shows on Fridays; I had to work my day job, and had to speed off early on Sundays to get back in time for work. I was so envious of everyone who just got to stay an extra day because it was their job. It was a great feeling to finally take that next step. Nowadays, Devil's Due has to turn down conventions, because there are simply too many to attend.

One of the most important things to do once you've made your initial contacts is follow-up. As you'll find, the more conventions you attend, the harder it is not to lose things on the trip home. This goes double for big publishers. When a convention is over, displays and inventory must be broken down and shipped in a very short amount of time, and it's very chaotic. Don't ever feel jilted if someone loses your information and never follows up with you: simply make an effort to be the person who does keep his or her collected information, and makes the first contact.

VISIBILITY AND CUSTOMER AWARENESS

Another benefit of conventions is, of course, interacting with hundreds, if not thousands of potential fans all in one room. There is nowhere else that you can find so many people that fall into your target market. You get to interact face to face with fans, sign comics, draw sketches, and of course, sell your merchandise.

Greater than that, though, is the ability to make sure that everyone simply notices you, and by you I mean your product. Whether they buy it at the show or not, you want them to walk away with your branding etched into their minds. That can make all of the difference when someone is perusing the racks at their local comic book store two months later, and they notice something familiar about your book, sitting on the rack. This is why you need to make sure you have an easy to read, eye-catching logo and image designed into your booth set-up. Let's imagine that you're attending a con (as we call them in the industry) with an attendance of 20,000 people. You can't expect all 20,000 attendees to buy your comics, but you should think of that as the equivalent of being able to advertise a full-page ad in a magazine with a 20,000 copy circulation. This is what I mean by "visibility."

Even if they don't buy a comic, try to make sure that everyone gets something. It may be a flyer, postcard, or sticker that directs them to your website. Check the previous volume of this series to find out more about marketing directly to the customers. I do not recommend giving away candy, as people tend to focus on the sweets, and not your comics.

You also have the chance to increase your visibility by advertising in the convention program pamphlets, or by sponsoring parties or auctions the organizers might set up. This can be pricey, but depending on the size of the show, and the flexibility of the management, you may be able to negotiate something that works within your budget.

When working with the convention organizers, always remember that running a show is extremely taxing on the brain, and coordinators are usually trying to appease ten people at a time. Just be patient, and state clearly if you have a problem while remaining very polite. That sounds like the obvious tip of the week, but so many people lose their cool in the chaos of setting up for a convention.

The last category in which you have a chance to score "visibility points" is the press. Many of the online comic book news and fan sites send reporters to all the major shows, and they're always looking for material. If you are fortunate enough to pass a review copy along to a reporter, or land an interview on, say, Newsarama.com, you just increased your visibility from 20,000 people to upwards of 100,000.

I guess what I'm saying is that you need to always think of the big picture, and not just get caught up in where you are right at that moment. That doesn't mean every convention is great, but you can get a lot out of a good one.

MEETINGS

A lot of the success you have at a convention revolves around the planning you do before the show, even moreso than the activities during the show itself. I mentioned press just a while ago; although you will often stumble upon opportunities by luck, try to contact reporters a couple of weeks prior to a con, and arrange to be formally interviewed. This way, you are guaranteed press, and you have time to find out what images or information would appeal the most to a particular journalist.

This is also a great opportunity to meet artists, writers, and anyone else you've been dealing with via the internet or over the phone. As I've said before, nothing compares to a face to face meeting, and conventions are where many relationships are formed.

Look closely at the programming. Is anyone from your distributor going to be there? Anyone from your printing company? Distributors and printers usually only attend very large shows, but you don't want to miss the opportunity to meet them. When you get outside of the comic book industry, and attend shows that cover other media, these meetings become more important. When I fly to a book industry trade show, I make sure that I have meetings scheduled with my distributor, and the buyers of any large chain stores that will be attending, as an opportunity to sell DDP product. Also, after you've been around for a few years, you'll know so many people that you have to schedule formal meetings just to get anything done.

Try to scope out the convention layout before these

appointments so you can determine the best place to meet, away from the chaos of the show where both parties can concentrate and hear each other. At a show like the one in San Diego, this is a challenge, but most are easy enough to manage.

I have a hard time walking from one end of a convention to another without running into three or four people that I haven't seen in months, who want to say hi. I always try to, but there simply isn't enough time in the weekend to talk to everyone at length. And no, it's not because of my super duper charm, it's simply because I've been around for so damn long. It's always good to be able to excuse yourself for a meeting, where you have time to get down to business. Meetings are also necessary at huge shows like the Comic-Con International: San Diego, because, well, good luck finding anyone if you don't have a scheduled appointment and a copy of their booth number.

With that said, it's awesome to know so many people from all over the world, and to have so many buddies under one roof. Some of the coolest experiences of my life have taken place over the span of a convention weekend.

SALES

Who likes to make money? Ah, of course… you do, and a convention is a great way to do it. Before you expect to walk out of the con with a fistful of Benjamins, though, be prepared for the expenses you'll incur as a part of attending the show. Once you add those costs up, you'll know how important it is to make the most of your "table time" when you get to sell to the attendees.

You always want to have a pleasant look on your face, and be nice to every single person that passes your table. Don't let anyone walk by your table and make eye contact without giving them a "what's up?" or "how's it going?" Anything to draw them in. People have a lot to see at a show, and if you don't draw their attention, someone else will. So often I see people sit at their booths, not saying a word to anyone. Sometimes people even come up to the table to peruse art or merchandise, and don't get so much as a "hi." This is completely ridiculous, and if you're too shy to say hello to potential customers, then you should see who else can run your shows for you. You wouldn't hire yourself to print your books without knowing how to run a press, would you? So you don't want to give people a bad vibe at a convention if you're just naturally shy or grumpy. You are the face of your company or comic book.

People go to conventions to have a good time. They pay to be there. When they approach your table, you want them to receive a warm greeting. It's an atmosphere of camaraderie, so be sure and treat everyone as a friend.

I've been told by dozens of people that I'm very hard to read… my face, not my comics. Well, that's an improvement from when people used to always tell me that I looked pissed off. It's just the way my face is built, I guess, but I have to make a serious effort to be conscious of that, especially when I'm speaking with readers or fans, lest they think I'm a grump. Know your strengths and weaknesses, and don't be too proud to improve upon the latter.

So, once you manage to snag a potential reader at your table, they're most likely going to ask you what your comic or manga is about. This is where the "hook" comes into play. If you don't have a good hook, you're going to have a lot of trouble earning a fanbase.

For example, the DDP comic book *Kore* is about *a man*

thrown into the world of Abaddon, a realm of fantasy. But Abaddon's magic has run dry, and the elves, dwarves, and wizards must learn to live as we do, and deal with huge changes in their social structure. Yet our protagonist seems to be a pure source of magic, and everyone wants a piece of him. (I'm told by our marketing staff that *tongue-in-cheek fantasy with a fairy strip club* works as an even better hook, but really, is that appropriate for this publication?)

These are hooks. Now, maybe you just hate fantasy, and there's nothing I can do to make you like my comic. That will inevitably happen with some people, but if you have a concise hook you can grab people in a split second, and that may be all the time you have.

An easy tactic is comparing your concept to something that is more recognizable. For instance, you could say your book is *like Lost meets the X-Files* or *A Christmas Carol meets The DaVinci Code.* Whatever makes sense, as long as your references are common knowledge to your demographic.

Reiterating the point that not everyone will like your comic, do not be offended if they pass on by. Even if you've been sitting at your table all weekend and haven't sold one comic, don't project your frustrations onto anyone. I see this all the time, and it's pointless. Some people just aren't going to be interested in what you have to offer, no matter how well done it may be… even if it's free!

Don't wait for someone to ask you what your title is about. Perhaps you could ask them if they've ever heard about it? If they haven't, it's a great opportunity to inform them. If they have, then you can go into more detail about your specific offerings.

ROOKIE MISTAKES AND PITFALLS

I think the biggest mistake rookie convention exhibitors make is setting their expectations too high. Many walk into a show expecting that everyone is going to like his or her comic or manga, and that sales will be great too. They believe that they will walk away with a fistful of cash in hand, and be off to the next convention. It rarely goes that way. It takes time to perfect your sales tactics, and find what works best for you. It also takes experience in dealing with convention organizers and shipping companies to make sure things go smoothly.

Conventions are also long and tiring, and it's easy to use up all of your energy on the first day. Make sure you bring plenty of water and something to snack on, or that you have enough money to pay for the over-inflated convention center food (I think they get their prices from the future or something). Otherwise you may be getting dizzy in the seventh or eighth hour of the show, especially if you overdid "Bar Con" the night before (I'll explain that fun experience later).

That said, going to your first show is a wonderful experience. It's your first chance to see what real flesh and blood people think of your comic book, not just faceless handles on a message board. People are usually never brutally honest to your face, but you'll know if you're onto something or not just by the response of people coming up to your booth and buying your product, or quickly walking by.

Be sure not to get taken by surprise by expenses that can arise. If you shipped merchandise to a show using Union Workers, you're going to get charged for any shipments brought to your booth unless delivered on a specific day arranged by the show organizers.

Also understand that the convention organizers are not the same organization that is working for the convention center. One is simply renting from the other, so you're dealing with multiple organizations.

Lastly, don't forget to remove your geek-badge after the show! In more politically correct terms, that means "remove your exhibitor badge."

MAJOR CONVENTIONS

The king of all comic conventions is the Comic-Con International: San Diego. Although it has arguably become more of a "pop culture" con than a comic con, due to all of the movie studios, toy companies and video game industry professionals in attendance, it's still growing every year, and is the show that everyone goes to. If you want to meet the highest caliber of industry pros, this is where you need to go. I'd go so far as to say, if you can only go to one convention all year, make it this one.

Wizard World

Founded by the publisher of *Wizard: The Guide to Comics* magazine, this company has built a pop-culture empire out of their shows. Now spanning across the nation, Wizard World, although pricey, has some of the best comic book conventions in the country. They currently have annual events in Chicago, Philadelphia, LA, and Dallas.

SPX: Small Press Expo

This convention is held once a year in Baltimore, Maryland, and focuses on the alternative side of comics. If you have a mainstream super-hero or fantasy title, this isn't the place to go, but if it's more slice-of-life, this is where you want to be.

APE: Alternative Press Expo

Although I've never attended, I've been told that APE is the West Coast equivalent of SPX, held once a year in California.

Wonder Con

This is another show I've never attended, but if you're on the West Coast, this is one of the larger conventions, held annually in Oakland, California.

Heroes Con

This show is held in Charlotte, North Carolina, and is known for its high caliber of artistic talent and intimate setting, although it's still a large show.

Motor City Con

If you're in the Midwest or Northeast, the Motor-City Con is one of the old standbys. They usually have a heavy amount of television stars and B-movie guests as well as the regular comic book fair.

Pittsburgh Comicon

I've been doing this show for a decade, and you couldn't encounter a nicer group of convention promoters. If you want to be treated right, despite having no track record in the industry, this is a great show, and it has a solid attendance. Pittsburgh also seems to draw a large horror-movie crowd too for some reason.

Mid-Ohio-Con

A small but fun show in Columbus, that has been going on for about twenty million years. Okay, about twenty. It always runs on the weekend after Thanksgiving, and although I haven't been in a couple of years, it was one of my main stops on the small press circuit. It's usually sponsored by the Laughing Ogre, one of the best comic book shops in the country which hosts a great party every Friday before the show.

There are also a number of smaller conventions throughout the country, probably in your own city. Take time to investigate these, and decide if they are worth your time to attend.

PREPARATION

The process of registering for and attending a convention can range anywhere from over six months to just a few short weeks. The more popular the show, the earlier you need to reserve your space. Besides the convention itself, you'll need to book hotels and make travel arrangements, and you usually get the best deals by doing so far in advance. In the case of the Comic-Con International: San Diego, hotels open up for availability on a certain day, about six months before the convention, and sell out within a matter of hours.

Regardless, there are a few important steps you must perform when attending any convention.

Registration

A simple process of completing application forms for table or booth space and determining how much space you want, and what it will cost. Some conventions insist on money at the time of registration, and others give you more time. Very few, if any, let you wait until the day of the show to pay so be sure to keep an eye on the deadlines.

Many conventions have registration deadlines that hit a few months before the shows, and the closer you get to the show date, the higher the price.

Hotel Reservations and Travel Arrangements

Once you have confirmed a space at the convention, the next step is booking your hotel and travel plans. You can actually book your hotel even if you're not sure you'll be attending a show, because you have up until a day or two before the show to cancel the reservations. You never pay any hotel expenses until the day of check out, so keep that in mind. You don't want to book a show only to find you have no place to sleep, although that's only an issue at the largest conventions.

Plane tickets are different. You're going to need to pay for those immediately, so I advise purchasing them as soon as possible after confirming your placement at a show.
Last is your car rental, if necessary. Again, you don't have to pay for your car rental until the day you return it, so I'd recommend reserving one as soon as you know you may be attending a specific con.

(Indy Small-Budget Trick: If your wallet is especially thin, one simple tactic is to use the cash you've made at the show to pay for your hotel and rental car. You'll still need a credit card to reserve them, but since payment isn't due until you're leaving, you can request to pay with cash. Of course, you need to have a "Plan B" if you don't make enough at the show to cover these expenses.)

Booth Design

I think this is one of the most exciting parts of the convention experience. Designing your booth display is your chance to show off your comic to the world, and make yourself stand out from everyone else.

It's a challenge, because you don't have a lot of space to work with, especially if you're in the small-press area, or what's commonly referred to as "artist alley." Your set-up can be as simple as 18x24 posters on easels placed behind you and a nice table skirt, or it can be as wild as your imagination and budget will allow you to be. Try attending a decent-sized convention and perusing other booths to get ideas before you attempt to do it on your own. Even today at Devil's Due it's common practice to take pictures of other company booth displays to brainstorm ideas for the following year.

Try to pick a booth display concept that is easily mobile, cheap to transport, and that contains images that you can use for an entire convention season. When I was starting out, I used to carry an elaborate set-up made out of PVC piping and cloth banners, with posters attached. It collapsed down into a big duffle bag and a few flat poster boxes, but it took forever to set up. Then, as Devil's Due grew, we created some extremely complicated booth displays. One was actually made of sheet metal, mesh fencing, and translucent plastic! It looked really cool, but damn if it didn't take hours to set up and cost a ton to ship. I resisted purchasing a profes- sional "pop-up booth," (the curved black back-drops you will see at any show), because they cost anywhere from $2,000 to $3,000, but I was paying more than that in shipping and labor costs. They collapse into two fairly small ship- ping barrels, with wheels attached for easy transport, and are worth every penny. Now we just build off of the pop-up booth format, and it takes a fraction of the time to set up.

I don't think you need a pop-up booth when you're just starting out, but if you start to grow, or if money's not the issue, I suggest getting one as soon as you can. To find these, check on Ebay for the best deals.

Inventory and Supply Planning

The most common mistake new publishers make is bringing too much inventory to a convention. Sure, it's better to have stock left over than it is to sell out on the first day of the show, but one small box holds a lot of comics. Although big publishers can sell hundreds of certain titles at a show, they often sell less than thirty or forty copies of specific issues.

If it's your first show, it's hard to calculate how many comics you'll need, how many sketches or pages of art you'll sell, or what the reaction to your book is going to be like. Just make your best educated guess, without losing an arm and a leg on shipping expenses, or without carrying around 500 pounds of comic book boxes all weekend, and adjust for the next time.

Shipping

Do not be caught off guard by the shipping restrictions and fees at a convention. Be sure to read the paperwork to find out if the show you're attending is fairly lax in their policies, or if they require union participation. This won't be a huge issue for someone publishing one small-press comic, but if you have a skid of boxes being delivered at a show like San Diego, you may be charged as much as a few hundred dollars extra if you don't read the fine print on the rules.

Set-Up (supply delivery)

As long as you can set up your display by yourself, or with one other person, you'll be fine at any show. If you get very ambitious, though, and require all kinds of tools and equipment to construct things, you may find a union supervisor assigning someone to help you, whether you want his help or not, all for a nice fee. Again, this is probably NOT an issue for anyone reading this, but it's always good to know.

The next time you're at a show, and you see those huge displays for companies like DC Comics, Sci-Fi Channel, or even Dark Horse, think about the fact that not only did they pay thousands of dollars to reserve the space, but all of that stuff had to be designed, manufactured and shipped, and the companies probably had to pay union help about $50 per person per hour to assemble it.

Breakdown

I'm always amazed at the breakdown process at a convention. After three or four days of insanity, walking around huge displays with loud music and flashing lights, no matter how enormous the set-up, it seems like everything disappears in a matter of seconds at the close of the show on the very last day. Within a few hours, this magical wonderland you've just spent the weekend living in will no longer exist. Anyway, my point is that when a show is over, it's time to get yourself in gear and get the heck out of the convention center.

On the days preceding that, though, when the show ends each night, you don't have a lot of time to pack your materials for the night. After a long day at a con, everyone wants to run out to the nearest restaurant or bar, and so will you most likely. Try to make a serious effort to head back to your hotel room and count your money, though, before you do. If you are comfortable doing it at the table, that's fine too, but just be sure to keep an accounting of it so when the show is over you have detailed information about how well the event went for you. It's very easy to spend that wad of cash in your pocket after a few drinks, or picking up the tab for someone else because you're feeling generous, only to discover in the morning that you should have clung to every penny.

On the final day of breakdown, even if your display doesn't take long to pack up, you're going to have to weave through everyone else that's breaking down and packing up. If you plan to ship materials home, rather than carry them, you'll need to arrange for that beforehand. It's very easy to bring FedEx or UPS forms along, and fill them out after you've packed up your materials, and then deliver them to the nearest drop off location. Most major convention centers and hotels offer FedEx and UPS service, but in the rare case that they don't, you don't want to be stuck driving boxes to a location in a town you're unfamiliar with, and still get to the airport on time (trust me, I know).

Resolve Billing Issues

This isn't something you usually need to worry about, but if you run into the situation where you do need to have skids delivered, and are paying the various unions and shipping companies to deliver skids to your booth (these are called **DRAYAGE CHARGES**), be sure to check whatever credit cards you may have used on the next few statements.

Sometimes charges magically appear that you should have never paid. For instance, at Devil's Due, we've flown people out a day early, and paid for the extra man hours and hotel fees just to take advantage of discounts offered if you set up your display on a certain date, only to be charged anyway. This leads to many phone calls pestering customer service managers to give the money back. In the end it usually works out, but causes added frustration. Be on the lookout that you're only paying what you owe.

BAR CON

When you attend a convention as a casual spectator, and you meet the artists, get signatures, and buy a bunch of cool merchandise, you might not know that you're only experiencing half of the con experience. Every convention has another side to it... a fun, and sometimes a little bit seedy phenomenon I like to call "Bar Con" (a phrase coined by DDP's Susan Bishop).

For the artists, retailers, and anyone else working the show floor, the official hours of the convention are only half of the experience. Where everyone really lets their hair down, has a good time, and forms the relationships that last throughout the years are at the dinners, parties, and spontaneous pub crawls that happen in the evenings. This is an industry where very few people work in big offices with dozens of employees to socialize with. Many creators work in their home, or in small studios, and never get to interact with their peers face to face, except at conventions. So when they do, everyone seems to be making up for lost time, playing catch up.

After you've done a full convention season, if you can pull it off, and hung out with the same people in half a dozen cities across the country, it's easy to feel like you've known them for years. I imagine it's a very tiny glimpse of what it's like traveling on a summer concert tour, without all the groupies beating down your door.

To female readers, I say that from a man's perspective, because let's face it, if you're a woman attending these shows, you probably will have to beat guys back with a stick—comparable to some touring rock star.

Be careful not to over-do the Bar Con experience, and lose sight of the fact that this is still business. You have to get up in the morning and make money, so be careful. If you party too much, you may find yourself doing something foolish, and burning bridges in the process, depending on who's around to witness the events. First impressions are the most important. After you've been around for a few years, then you can make an ass out of yourself.

Seriously, though, let me clarify that this does not mean you have to actually go to parties, do shots and get plastered, but it does mean that you should be interacting with people after the shows. Don't just go retreat in your hotel room every night reading comics that you bought at the show that day. That's fine for the average attendee, but you're trying to network here, so take advantage of it.

If you're serious about breaking into this industry, and you're not taking part in any Bar Con events, I really feel you're missing out.

RETAILER CONTACTS

The people you'll meet at Bar Con come from every level of the comic industry ladder, but you need to target each category specifically to maximize your networking. By simply exhibiting, you're hitting your first demographic – the readers. Bar Con is probably the best way to meet artists and writers, aside from scheduled meetings, or simply being their "booth neighbor" all weekend. Retailers are usually in a separate area of the convention than the publishers, though, so you'll need to make extra effort to promote your title to them.

Take note that not every retailer at a convention has a comic book store. Many of them only sell golden or silver age comics (comic books that were published years ago), so they're not going to be interested in buying yours. Look for the displays that are offering modern comics, and keep an eye out for those representing an entire chain of stores. If you don't know who these people are, you'll have to learn by talking to them.

The retailers are usually very busy at these shows, and don't have a lot of time to talk, so keep your discussions short and sweet. Make a small flyer or give them any other simple promotional material you have, or better yet, a sample comic; but don't expect them to manage to take it home. 95% of the time they will *lose* this by the end of the first day, because conventions are crazy. You're only giving it to them so that the next time they see an ad for your book, there's a better chance they'll recognize it, and hopefully place an order. This is why you want to get their business cards or addresses, so that you may follow up with them later.

CLOSING

When you've been doing something for so long it's easy to leave important chunks of information out that, although simple, may be imperative to understanding the chain of instructions that follow. I hope I didn't do that to anyone.I also hope I've raised many questions in your minds. There's nothing better than thinking of a question that you previously never even knew you should have asked. When that happens to me, I know it means I'm actually learning something new.

So whether you are a die-hard aspiring self-publisher, or if you're just a casual reader interested in what goes on behind the scenes of this capes-and-tights industry, thanks for checking out the series.

For those of you who are serious: get out there and start working on your game plan. Just don't do too good of a job and become my competition five years from now.

SELLING YOUR COMICS TO HOLLYWOOD

One of the main reasons a lot of people self-publish comics today is for the potential development of their comic book into other media such as film, television, and video games. If you get into publishing solely to do this, you're probably going to burn out before you really have a chance to make it. Remember, the process of publishing a comic takes months or even years, so the only way to be truly successful at it is to have a genuine love of comics, first and foremost. Otherwise, there are better ways to try to break into the film and video game industries.

That said, if you are going to self-publish, it makes perfect sense to make your comic as TV/film/game friendly as possible, maximizing the potential you have for building your property's popularity and possibly even making some nice coin off of the deal. The chances of actually getting a film made are slim to none, but hey, if movies exist then that means *someone* is getting paid to make them. Why not you?

Success is all about hard work, timing, and luck. More often than not success boils down to positioning yourself so that luck can more easily find you. For example, Devil's Due has the horror-comedy series *Hack/Slash* in development for film with Rogue Pictures. The studio executives totally understand the property, we have a great relationship with the co-writer and director, and things just seem to be moving along almost too well. This success can be attributed to nothing but luck, some weird alignment of the planets. If it continues to go so smoothly, we'll be completely spoiled by this experience. However, this is after almost three years of shopping the property around to various Hollywood and video game studios. Almost every major player in town rejected Hack/Slash before finding a studio that "got it;" the title was just a few steps beyond what studios wanted from a horror film. Horror at that time was very serious, like *Saw* or *The Grudge*, but now you're already starting to see more old school style "slasher" flicks being announced for development.

We previously had other directors and talent attached, and almost had *Hack/Slash* set up a number of times, all falling through. Meanwhile, the comic book was a cult phenomenon. The comic didn't exactly make us money hand over fist, but the people who did like it, *really* liked it. Had we given up, no one would have blamed us, but we stuck to our guns, and eventually Lady Luck arrived.

WHAT'S THE FIRST STEP?

So, you're serious about pitching your property to film studios and video game companies, but don't have a clue how. You'll need to find someone who does. Although some people don't feel they need one, an agent or a manager can greatly aid you in your quest for a studio deal. An agent simply represents you, putting you in touch with people you need to meet in order to sell yourself, and helps negotiate deals when you manage to pull it off. An agent cannot be attached to your deal in any other way, unlike a manager, who usually becomes attached as a producer. The reason for this, very simply, is because producers get paid more. In many cases, your manager's producer fee may even be higher than your fee for the sale of the film rights, depending on what the manager has produced in the past.

Managers take a more active role in the development of your property. They help you tweak your idea to better suit other mediums, help you develop your "Story Bible," streamline your "take" (the short pitch you'll be giving in your meetings) and, if you don't live where movies are actually made, the manager can attend for you.

I don't claim to be a seasoned veteran in the world of film and video games yet, so take what I say with a grain of salt, but I found the best way to go about it was to start with a more hands on manager. Keep your agreement with them to a relatively short amount of time, not locking you into anything with them for more than a year. You can always renew the contract if things are going well. As you begin to learn more about the industries, you can continue to work with the manager, but also use other representation. Devil's Due is currently represented by William Morris Agency, one of the larger talent agencies in Los Angeles, and we still work closely with our former creative managers who are now producing the *Hack/Slash* film with Rogue Studios and helping set up the video game deals.

Going into the future, Devil's Due is now in a better position to attach itself as a producer on new projects, giving us more creative control as well as a bigger paycheck. In the entertainment industry, it's all about what you did on your last deal, so the first one's always the hardest hurdle to get over.

WHERE DO I FIND ONE OF THESE GUYS?

I admit that I lucked out and Hollywood came knocking on my door before I had to go looking for it, thanks to the success of Devil's Due. Since then, producers, screenwriters and studio execs have approached me countless times via email or through comic conventions (mostly Comic-Con International: San Diego). This is another benefit of exhibiting at major conventions that I didn't include when writing the earlier chapter, "Hit the Pavement". Once you launch your product out in the market, don't be surprised if you get one of these emails. The problem is, unless it's a huge name on the other line, you have no way of knowing if the person approaching you is a major player or just some guy in an apartment trying to latch onto a comic book property because they're the current rage, so do your research. IMDB.com is a great place to get information.

The best way of locating an agent or manager is by word of mouth. After you've done a few shows or gotten to know more comic creators, ask around and see if anyone has any referrals. These days a number of creators have representation in Hollywood, so it should be easier than it sounds to find some names.

THE STORY BIBLE

So let's say you've found your representation, or even decided to go without it, and you're ready to start sending your comics to the studios.

For your pitch, you'll need to compile a **STORY BIBLE**, which is a binder containing all of the elements that potential buyers will have questions about when considering a purchase for film rights. I find that doing these actually helps create better comic books; forming a bible forces you to fix any kinks that you may have left open in your story.

First and foremost, as in any submission, you must give them the hook.

I discussed the hook in the marketing section of this book, but let me reemphasize that it is the most important aspect of your comic. What is it about your story that makes someone immediately interested in it? What makes your comic stand out from the other hundreds of titles on the market? Now sum that up in only a few sentences. Sometimes deals are done based on the hook alone, but what's realistically going to happen, if you're lucky, is that your hook will make a studio executive want to read through the rest of your bible.

It happens that quickly. You have just a few seconds to capture their interest and they know immediately if your idea is a pass or go and ready for round two. This is when it's time to examine whether or not your idea is as film-friendly or game-friendly as possible. For instance, at Devil's Due we decided that out of all of our comic book properties, *Hack/ Slash* was the best one to focus on for our first movie deal, because it was very grounded. Horror is usually inexpensive to film, and almost always makes its money back in the first few weekends of theatrical release, so we knew it would be the most palatable to studios. Our comic book *Kore* was something that would require a huge budget, and also starred a monster as the main character, which usually doesn't fly in Hollywood, so we knew it would be a much harder sell.

If you're serious about selling your comic book property to a film studio or television network, you should think about how to keep it as grounded in reality as possible.

After the hook, you should follow with a more detailed plot breakdown of your comic series. It's not necessary that your comic run in short story arcs, but keep in mind that studios will want to know how your concept can fit into a two-hour film, and what stories could provide sequels as well. Your plot shouldn't be too over detailed. Keep it down to a few pages, and if they like what they see they'll ask for more.

Overall, you want your proposal to look professional and include eye-catching graphics, which shouldn't be too hard considering you'll have dozens of pages of artwork.

CHARACTER BIOS are the next item necessary for any story bible. There are no official rules that say they must come before or after your plot breakdown, but I prefer to provide them afterwards. I try to look at it from the studio execs' perspective. They have stacks and stacks of pitches to read, so what are they going to do first? Read the hook. If that grabs the execs' interest, then they'll want to know more about the plot breakdown. If it doesn't, in the garbage your story bible goes. If the plot breakdown grabs them, then great, finally they will want to read more about the characters, and then the world they live in, and if applicable, the gadgets they use.

I save **ENVIRONMENTS** and **GADGETS/TECH** for last, except in the rare occasion that a city or place is a character in and of itself. For example, if you were pitching *Sin City*, the dingy town is just as much a character element as Marv or Nancy.

If you have one, your manager should review your bible before it is sent out to the studios. The manager should also be involved in the bible's crafting.

Obviously bringing your comic to film or video games is a lot more complicated than something that can be explained in one chapter of a book, but hopefully this at least gets you moving in the right direction, and asking the right questions. Maybe at the end of the day you'll decide that you don't care about selling your comic to Hollywood, and that you just want to create a comic for comics' sake; after all, if you're in it for the right reason, that's the way it should be. If you're serious about selling your concept, good luck. Just don't beat me to it!

APPENDIX
Useful Forms

HOW TO READ A PRINTING INVOICE

"Terms" identifies the amount of time you have to pay your bill. Some printers will demand payment in advance, but if you have solid credit, you should be able to arrange for 30 day payment terms—also known as "NET 30." In this example the option is also given to pay within 10 days of receipt, and receive a 2% discount.

FACTURE - INVOICE

MONTRE-ALL PRINT

Invoice number (sometimes called "Job number") is the number the printer will use to identify this specific job. Be sure to refer to it in all correspondence with the printer. This will ensure you appear organized and professional, as well as minimize the potential for accounting and shipping errors.

VENDU À/SOLD TO:

DEVIL'S DUE PUBLISHING INC.
461
SUI   OD
CHI
606

Your business address shows up here. I've already claimed this one!

Nº FACTURE - INVOICE NO.

Nº DU CLIENT - CUSTOMER'S NO.

COMMANDE Nº - YOUR ORDER NO.

DE TRAVAIL/JOB #   DATE D'EXPÉDITION/SHIPPING DATE

MOIS / JOUR / ANNÉE 01/27/05	T.P.S. / G.S.T.	LIC. PROV. LIC.	TERMES - TERMS 2% 10 DAYS, NET 30	VENDEUR - SALESMAN 007

HERO WORSHIP #1
32 pg B&W

This is the title of your job—for our purposes, your book will be known as "Hero Worship." In this case, you've requested a quote for a 32 page, black and white comic. with color cover.

5,000 COPIES

*4,000.00

ALL PRICES IN U.S. FUNDS

SHIPPING

500.00

TOTAL

US $ 4,500.00
==============

*Prices are not an accurate representation of printing costs. Consult a printer for actual costs. This is a sample invoice for educational pruposes only. The author and publisher recommend consulting legal and accounting advice from a registered and licensed professional before publishing. This and other forms are adapted from existing forms; some information has been altered, deleted or simplified for illustrative purposes.

HOW TO READ A PRINTER QUOTE

Binding commonly comes in 2 formats: *Saddle-Stitched*, which means stapled, like most 32pg comics; or *Perfect Bound*, which has a spine, more like a traditional book.

4/4 represents the 4 ink colors used in the printing process (4-color printing = full color printing), on each side of the paper. 4/1 would mean 4 color on one side, and 1 color (probably black) on the other side of the paper. *1/1* means a black & white book.

This number is how the printer identifies this specific job. Since they negotiate prices with each customer, your rate may differ from someone else's, thus making this number vital to tracking.

Bleed means that the art goes right up to the page edge. Covers are almost always full bleed; interiors don't have to be full bleed—but if you want even 1 page of your comic to bleed off the edge, then your whole book will be considered *full bleed*.

RE-ALL PRINT
QUOTATION

Date :

Quotation # : **2063-3-JL**

These are your print dimensions. *Make sure* the book is the size you want.

Customer :

Title :   HERO WORSHIP #1

We are pleased to present our quotation for the production of the above title.

Size :	Final	: 5" x 7 1/2" Open size : 10" x 7 1/2"
Pages :	Inside	: 144 pages
	Cover	: 4 pages
Printing :	Inside	: 1/1 bleed
	Cover	: 4/4 bleed + U.V. gloss 1 side
Paper :	Inside	: Windsor Offset # 2 Smooth Finish 60 Lbs
	Cover	: Carolina C1C 12 Pts
Binding :	Perfect bound	
Material supplied :	Disk Syquest Quark-X-Press in design Macintosh	
(by customer)	Proofs supplied	
Packing :	In cartons on skids	
Currency :	All in U.S. funds	
Tolerance :	+ ou - 2 %	
Price :	Valid for a thirty days period	

This is your *page count*. Comics pages are printed in groups of 8, meaning you must have 24 pgs, 32 pgs, 40 pgs, etc. Standard size is 32 pgs for a $2.95 book. Your cover is considered an additional 4 pgs: Front, Inside Front, Inside Back, and Back.

This is the *kind* of paper used. Ask your printer for samples.

How your comics will be shipped. A *skid* is one forklift pallet.

Total Quantity :	1,000	3,000	5,000	10,000
Total Price :	$3500	$5500 $6500	$8000	
Price / 1000's :				
Add'l / 1000's :				

Total Quantity :	15000	20000
Total Price :	$9500	$10,500
Price / 1000's :		
Add'l / 1000's :		

As your print quantity goes up, the cost per unit goes down considerably!

Price confirmations are subject to paper price and availability effective at time of order.

Printing presses are so complex and fast-moving that they work in approximate quantities. This disclaimer allows the printer to charge you 2% more or less, based on the quantity they print.

_____ntative

Customer signature

_____
Date

...owledge having read the terms and conditions set forth on the above and accept ...constituting the printing contract.

HOW TO READ A
PURCHASE ORDER

This is the P.O.#. It is what you use for all invoicing. Note that we include the P.O.# as on the Distributor Invoice.

P U R C H A S E   O R D E R   # 125621

SHIP TO:

Please ship to location(s) listed below

INVOICE TO:

TAM COMIC DISTRIBUTORS
Attn: Accounts Payable

ISSUED TO:

Your company contact info here.

Agreed upon payment terms. In this example, the distributor will pay you within 30 days of receiving comics.

This is where to send your invoice. It's a good idea to fax or email *and* send via snail mail.

ISSUE DATE   TERMS
11/25/05   NET 30

NOTE: Ship as ready. Please include purchase order number on all shipments and invoices
This order is subject to the purchase order terms on file with your company. Refer to such terms in the placement of this order.

LN 0001: HERO WORSHIP #1
    NOTE: INITIAL ORDER FULFILLMENT

ITEM NO: AUG05335   PROD ID: PLEASE PROVIDE
RETAIL PRICE: $2.95
UNIT PRICE: $1.18
IN STORE DATE: 10/26/05   CANCEL DATE: 12/09/05

When your book is scheduled to arrive in stores.

Please ship the qty listed to location(s) below
        QTY
        2,000 Salem W'house
TOTAL QTY 2,000   COST: $2360

SUMMARY TOTAL QTY 2,000   COST: $2360

Total number of comics you'll be shipping.

Price you'll be paid for each copy, usually *60% off* your retail price. In this case, your book is retailing for $2.95. $2.95 x 40% = $1.18.

Total price you'll be paid. 1000 comics x 40% = $1180.

A breakdown of how many copies are to be sent to each distributor warehouse. There may be several, and it's important for your printer to receive this info for shipping.

This is the number the distributor assigns to your comic for that specific issue. When you *invoice* them, be sure to refer to this number.

Date the distributor can *CANCEL* the order if comics aren't received.

INVOICING THE DISTRIBUTORS

Include the corresponding numbers from your Purchase Order here.

State the agreed-upon amount of days the customer has to pay you.

Every communication about this book should include the Invoice Number. You will generate this # yourself.

Your address.

Invoice

Date	Invoice #

Bill To

Include customer's name, address and phone number here.

Include extra info space to identify what you're charging for if necessary, such as a project #. This doesn't always apply, though.

P.O. No.	Terms	Project
125621	NET 30	

Description	Qty	Rate	Amount
AUG05335 HERO WORSHIP #1	2,000	1.18	$2360
	# of comics the distributor ordered.	Cost you are charging distributor per copy (in dollars)	

This is the Item Number. Item Nos are attached to your title/issue much like the Purchase Order Number.

List the project you're charging for here. Every issue of every title should be listed separately—*never* group orders for multiple items under the same listing.

Do you owe this distributor money, or do they owe you from a previous invoice? Include that info here. For this example, we'll pretend they owe us $500.

Total	$2360
Payments/Credits	$ 500
Balance Due	$2860

Prices are not an accurate representation of printing costs. Consult a printer for actual costs. This is a sample invoice for educational purposes only. The author and publisher recommend consulting legal and accounting advice from a registered and licensed professional before publishing. This and other forms are adapted from existing forms; some information has been altered, deleted or simplified for illustrative purposes.

BASIC ROYALTY REPORT

Ninja Pants: Issue 1: Invoice

Retail Price	$2.95		Date: xx/xx/xx
Wholesale Cos	$1.18		Date of last report: xx/xx/xx

	QTY	COST	Income
Qty Printed	4000		
Copies Sold via Distributor X	1700	$1.18	$2,006.00
Copies Sold online	362	$2.95	$1,067.90
Copies Sold via Conventions	368	$2.95	$1,085.60
Promotional/Give-away copies	100 $	-	$ -
Totals	2530		$4,159.50
Total Inventory Left	1470		

Expenses

Printing	$2,000
Shipping	$540
Advertising	$1,000
Total Expenses	$3,540

Net Sales from Book	$619.50
Artist Royalty (50%)	$309.75

PRESS RELEASE

Emanuel Estrada
VP Marketing
(773) 657-6557
estrada@devilsdue.net
www.devilsdue.net

Devil's Due Publishing (DDP) Press Release

For Immediate Release

DEVIL'S DUE TO PUBLISH HACK/SLASH: SLICE HARD 25-CENT SPECIAL
Your mom would burn it if she knew you had it!

Chicago, IL – April 1, 2006 –Cassie Hack is trapped! Barred within a secret facility built solely to house dreaded hordes of Slashers, Cassie and Vlad must fight to survive! HACK/SLASH: SLICE HARD 25-CENT SPECIAL (DIAMOND CODE) tells how the two Slasher hunters ended up behind locked doors, and is the perfect jumping on point for the casual comic reader anticipating the still far-off HACK/SLASH feature film release! The SLICE HARD 25-CENT SPECIAL, written by creator Tim Seeley (FORGOTTEN REALMS, Loaded Bible) with artwork by Katie de Sousa, featuring 5pgs of original story, 3pgs of Cassie's origin, and 6pgs of SLICE HARD sketches, kicks off the newest HACK/SLASH miniseries, and introduces brand new character Acid Angel, a club girl Slasher who *loves* to drench innocents in acid!

"SLICE HARD not only features the first appearance of Acid Angel," proclaims Tim Seeley, "but is an awesome time to get in on the hilarious blood-bath of fun before the feature film ever hits theaters!"

"The SLICE HARD 25-CENT SPECIAL has a sure recipe for comic book success," says Devil's Due President Josh Blaylock. "One part Tim Seeley, one p~~art Katie de Sousa~~, add blood and guts... stir."

View Covers Here:

HACK/SLASH – SLICE ~~HARD~~ ... E) - ...ages of a comic book is coming in August, and Devil's Due
It's coming...The biggest HACK/SLASH event that has ~~over gra~~... is giving you a little peak. When Cassie Hack and Vlad the blade-wielding behemoth start stalking the newest slasher in their lineup of crazy killers, it's not long before the tables are turned, and they become the hunted! Acid Angel: the sexy slasher with a secret is unlike any villain they have fought before.

With a full story, and secret behind the scenes info, HACK/SLASH – SLICE HARD 25-CENT SPECIAL is the prelude the HACK/SLASH – SLICE HARD coming this August. Having a 25-cent cover price makes this issue a perfect jumping point for new readers, and a collector's must have.

HACK/SLASH: EUTHANIZED (FEB042289)
HACK/SLASH: GIRLS GONE DEAD (Cover A AUG042658, Cover B AUG042659)
HACK/SLASH: COMIC BOOK CARNAGE (JAN052620)
HACK/SLASH VS. EVIL ERNIE (Cover A APR052801, Cover B APR052802)
HACK/SLASH: LAND OF LOST TOYS #1 (OF 3) (SEP052896)
HACK/SLASH: LAND OF LOST TOYS #2 (OF 3) (OCT052930)
HACK/SLASH: LAND OF LOST TOYS #3 (OF 3) (Cover A NOV052892, Cover B NOV052893)

We encourage you to run, not walk to your retailer and reserve your copy today. To find a retailer call 1-888-COMIC-BOOK.

Devil's Due: Reminding everyone that pop culture IS our culture.

ABOUT DEVIL'S DUE PUBLISHING –
Devil's Due Publishing was formed in 1999 as both a commercial art studio and a small press comic book publisher. DDP's first breakout success was 2001's revamp of G.I. JOE, returning the long-lost 1980s characters to comics. Fans bought over 100,000 copies per month, immediately propelling G.I. JOE to the top of the charts. Today, DDP's lineup includes Forgotten Realms, Dragonlance, G.I. Joe: America's Elite, FAMILY GUY, eigoManga, Hack/Slash, Capcom's Killer 7, Monkey Pharmacy's Elsinore, the newly resurrected Chaos! Comics, and indie comics' magazine Lo-Fi.

###